FOLLOWING IN THE FOOTSTEPS
OF THE
PRINCES
IN THE TOWER

FOLLOWING IN THE FOOTSTEPS OF THE

PRINCES IN THE TOWER

ANDREW BEATTIE

PEN & SWORD
HISTORY

AN IMPRINT OF PEN & SWORD BOOKS LTD.
YORKSHIRE - PHILADELPHIA

First published in Great Britain in 2019 by
Pen and Sword History
An imprint of
Pen & Sword Books Ltd
Yorkshire - Philadelphia

ISBN 978 1 52672 785 5

A CIP catalogue record for this book is available from the British Library.

Typeset in Ehrhardt MT Std 11.5/14 by
Aura Technology and Software Services, India

Printed and bound in the UK by TJ International Ltd.

Pen & Sword Books Ltd incorporates the Imprints of Pen & Sword Books
Archaeology, Atlas, Aviation, Battleground, Discovery, Family History, History,
Maritime, Military, Naval, Politics, Railways, Select, Transport, True Crime,
Fiction, Frontline Books, Leo Cooper, Praetorian Press, Seaforth Publishing,
Wharncliffe and White Owl.

For a complete list of Pen & Sword titles please contact

PEN & SWORD BOOKS LIMITED
47 Church Street, Barnsley, South Yorkshire, S70 2AS, England
E-mail: enquiries@pen-and-sword.co.uk
Website: www.pen-and-sword.co.uk

or

PEN AND SWORD BOOKS
1950 Lawrence Rd, Havertown, PA 19083, USA
E-mail: Uspen-and-sword@casematepublishers.com
Website: www.penandswordbooks.com

Contents

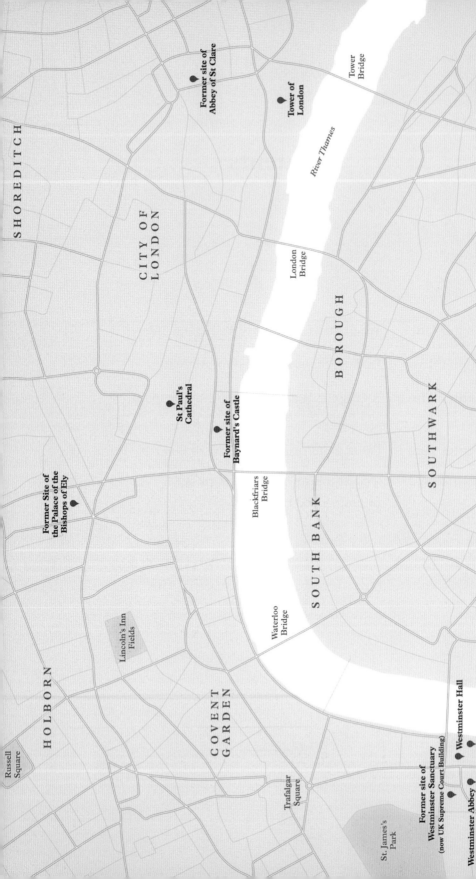

Louvain

Mechelen

Antwerp

Brussels

Bruges

Sandwich

Dover

Canterbury

Ashford

Eastwell

Colchester

Eltham

Hornsey

St Albans

Dunstable

Reading Windsor

Milton Keynes

Northampton Grafton

Oxford

Newark

Leicester

Stony Stratford

Sheriff Hutton

York

Market Bosworth

Minster Lovell

Pontefract

Leeds

Coventry

Middleham

Lichfield

Birmingham

Worcester

Gloucester

Manchester

Great Malvern

Shrewsbury

Wroxeter

Much Wenlock

Bewdley

Little Malvern

Bristol

Ludlow

Chester

Hereford

Wigmore

Southampton

Coldridge

Exeter

Introduction

In *The Daughter of Time*, the 1951 novel by the celebrated crime and mystery writer Josephine Tey, a cynical, soon-to-be-retired police officer named Alan Grant, recovering in hospital from an operation, decides to use his experience as a criminologist to investigate one of the most notorious supposed crimes in history: whether or not King Richard III was guilty of the murder of his two young nephews, Edward and Richard Plantagenet, the boys known as 'The Princes in the Tower'. He starts off with some detailed reading about the Wars of the Roses, the fifteenth-century civil wars that reached a conclusion soon after the princes' disappearance. Grant 'tried to make head or tail' of the wars, Tey tells us, but 'he failed. Armies marched and counter-marched. York and Lancaster succeeded each other as victors in a bewildering repetition. It was as meaningless as watching a crowd of dodgem cars bumping and whirling at a fair.'

In many ways the hapless Inspector Grant was barking up the wrong tree, in his emphasis on the Wars of the Roses as a key to understanding the fate of the princes. Although this long, complex and bloody conflict undoubtedly shaped the events that led to their imprisonment and disappearance, their ultimate fate was the result of a power struggle within one of the warring families – the House of York – rather than yet another episode of the in-fighting between the rival Houses of York and Lancaster. Inspector Grant really only needed to absorb a brief understanding of the Wars of the Roses to appreciate the historical context to Richard III seizing the throne in 1483 and possibly murdering his nephews.

Such a summary might run something like this: The Wars of the Roses erupted in 1455 as a response to the weak rule of King Henry VI, which revived interest in the rival claims to the throne of a nobleman, Richard, the third Duke of York (the grandfather of the princes in the Tower). The two opposing factions became known as the House of Lancaster (as Henry VI was a descendant of John of Gaunt, the First Duke of Lancaster and the third surviving son of Edward III) and the House of York (as Richard of York was descended from Edmund Langley, first Duke of York, the fourth surviving son of Edward III). Historians also point to the social and financial legacy of the Hundred Years War, which saw many English nobles disaffected by the loss of their holdings in continental Europe, as a contributory cause of the wars.

The conflict dragged on for thirty years. In the opening stages Richard, Duke of York's son, Edward, Earl of March, the princes' father, defeated and imprisoned Henry VI and was crowned Edward IV. Nine years later in 1470 the situation was reversed when Edward was deposed by Henry's Lancastrian forces. Edward swiftly regained control of the crown from Henry, imprisoned him and possibly ordered his murder, and then ruled until his own somewhat untimely death in 1483. The crisis that engulfed the princes came as a result of arguments concerning Edward IV's will, and who should rule during the minority of his son, Edward V, who acceded to the throne at the age of just 12. Of the two factions – Edward IV's widow Elizabeth on one side, and his brother Richard, Duke of Gloucester on the other – Richard emerged as eventual victor, and was crowned King Richard III, having declared, Edward V and his younger brother Richard – by then languishing in the Tower of London – barred from the throne as a result of their supposed illegitimacy. Richard III's brief rule ended just two years later, when a new Lancastrian claimant, Henry Tudor, defeated him at the Battle of Bosworth Field, which brought the thirty-year conflict to its conclusion. By that time the two princes had disappeared from public view.

Whether they were murdered – by Richard III, by his successor Henry VII, or by agents acting for these monarchs with or without their blessing, or whether one or both survived to assume a new identity in adulthood – is the subject of many books. But not this one. It is not difficult to see why authors and commentators from the 1480s onwards have attempted to claim (definitively) that they know what happened to the princes: the circumstances surrounding their disappearance remain the most compelling mystery in English history. Alison Weir, whose 1992 book *Richard III and the Princes in the Tower* firmly pins the blame on Richard III, considers the princes' fate to be 'a tale rich in drama, intrigue, treason, plots, judicial violence, scandal and infanticide … a mystery, a moral tale, and – above all – a gripping story.' At the heart of this story is the 'boy king', Edward V, who reigned more briefly than any English king since the Norman Conquest: just twenty-seven days, from 10 April to 25 June 1483. His coronation was twice postponed and he was never crowned. Although we cannot say anything with certainty about his death, we know much more about him than any other boy of his time. Moreover, he and his younger brother have been cast by history as symbols rather than living, breathing beings. They have been portrayed as innocent lives caught up in a deadly game of power politics, by a host of historians, biographers, playwrights and novelists – beginning with Thomas More (Richard III's first biographer) and William Shakespeare (whose play *Richard III* drew heavily from More's biography).

A survey and discussion of how novelists and playwrights have depicted the lives of the two princes, and have told the story of their imagined fates, is one aim of this book. Moreover, though, this book seeks to look at the princes' story in a way that has not been considered before: through the places associated with them during their lives. They were the sons of a reigning monarch and one of them became a monarch himself. Not surprisingly they grew up in castles and palaces and their lives are commemorated in a number of churches. Although some places associated with them are now gone – such as the monastery in Shrewsbury where Prince Richard was born, and the Palace of Westminster in London where both of them were brought up, at various stages of their lives – many locations survive, most particularly the Tower of London, where they were imprisoned, Ludlow Castle in Shropshire, where Edward Plantagenet spent much of his life, and Westminster Abbey, where a tomb inscribed with their names purports to be their place of burial. Whilst this book does not seek to shed any new or radical light on the princes' fate, it is hoped that through accounts of the places associated with them – from London and Kent to Shropshire, the English Midlands, and modern-day Belgium – a greater understanding of their lives and legacy can be gleaned.

Chapter One

Westminster: Sanctuary, Palace and Abbey

In the Middle Ages – as now – Westminster lay at the heart of English politics. Its royal palace was where parliament sat and where the monarch – who underwent an elaborate anointing ceremony known as a coronation, in the adjacent Abbey – presided over his court. Not surprisingly, in a story of political intrigue and the ruthless pursuit of ultimate power, Westminster crops up time and again in the story of the Princes in the Tower. Edward Plantagenet, the older of the two princes, was born here – or, more specifically, in the part of the abbey precincts that provided sanctuary for those in peril, which was the situation that had befallen his mother in November 1470 at the time of his birth. He then lived in the neighbouring Palace of Westminster until his household was removed to Ludlow in Shropshire when he was 3 years old. For the rest of his life he made frequent visits to the palace, when he would have been reunited with his younger brother Richard, whose permanent home this was. Today the palace's great hall (now known as Westminster Hall) is the best-known remaining part of the great palace of England's medieval kings. But a lesser-known part that remains is the undercroft of St Stephen's Chapel, the church that played host to one of the more extraordinary events in the lives of the two princes, namely the wedding of 4-year-old Richard Plantagenet to his equally young bride, Anne Mowbray. As for Westminster Abbey itself, it is the place of burial not only of the princes – though there's a great deal of scepticism as to whether the remains in their tomb are actually who they claim to be – but also a number of others directly or indirectly connected with their lives. These include their sister Elizabeth, her husband Henry VII, who some claim was their murderer; Edward Plantagenet's chamberlain

The magnificent western facade of Westminster Abbey dates from the mid eighteenth century. The arched windows of the medieval Jerusalem Chamber, where Edward Plantagenet was probably born, are visible bottom right.

Sir Thomas Vaughan; Richard's marriage partner, Anne Mowbray; and Thomas Millyng, the abbot of Westminster who gave Edward's mother sanctuary when she gave birth, and whose residence adjacent to the Abbey was known as Cheyneygates.

Cheyneygates: the birth of Edward Plantagenet in 1470

In September 1464, King Edward IV gathered his most prominent nobles around him at the great abbey at Reading, some forty miles west of London. At that time Reading Abbey, a foundation of King Henry I, was one of the great religious houses of England; today its ruins lie a short walk away from the shops and offices at the heart of this busy but rather bland county town. Once the king was sat in front of the nobles, he made the shocking announcement that he had recently married.

His new bride was a woman named Elizabeth Woodville; her family were minor Northamptonshire gentry. The announcement drew gasps of surprise from the assembled nobles, for more than one reason. First, the wedding had taken place in relative secrecy. Second, not only was the king's new bride of comparatively low birth, she was also a Lancastrian whose first husband, Sir John Grey of Groby, had been killed fighting at Towton some three years previously (in what was possibly the largest pitched battle ever fought on English soil). For months prior to this shock announcement, the king's powerful cousin, Richard Neville, Earl of Warwick, known as the 'kingmaker', had been beavering away behind the scenes to arrange for Edward to marry a foreign princess – namely Bona of Savoy, sister-in-law to the King of France. Now, with King Edward's announcement, Warwick had been humiliated. The wound cut deep – and then cut deeper over the years that followed, as the king continued to sideline Warwick. Seething at Edward's secrecy and the lightning-fast rise of the upstart Woodvilles, in the summer of 1469 Warwick forged an alliance with Edward's power-hungry brother George, Duke of Clarence. The two men gathered a force of mercenaries together on the continent and sailed with them to England, engaging Edward at Edgecote, fought just to the southwest of Northampton – at which the king, remarkably, was taken prisoner, and was then kept in a succession of castles. Warwick had it put about that Edward was the illegitimate son of an English archer, named Blaybourne, and that this meant he had no right to the throne, and in an act of vindictiveness towards the queen and her family he also had Elizabeth's father and brother beheaded.

Warwick found that he could not rule through an imprisoned king, and trouble on the Scottish border forced him to release Edward in early 1470. But he was not finished yet: in March of that year Warwick orchestrated another outbreak of violence that culminated in his defeat at Empingham in the East Midlands. He fled to France with Clarence and began to plot another invasion of England – this time with a major twist: Warwick was now siding with the Lancastrians. His aim was to see his hated foe Edward deposed, and the restoration to power of the former Lancastrian king Henry VI, who had been a prisoner in the Tower of London since 1464. When news reached London of the planned invasion, Queen Elizabeth was pregnant and it was vital that she sought out a place of safety in which to give birth. 'Be brave … be a queen,' her husband King Edward tells her in Philippa Gregory's novel *The White Queen* – Elizabeth being the 'white queen' of the title (an allusion to the white rose emblem of the House of York). 'Go to the Tower with the girls and keep yourself safe,' he continues. 'Then I can fight and win and come home to you.' The invasion duly came on 13 September 1470, by which time Elizabeth had indeed moved into the palatial royal apartments in the Tower of London. Within a couple of weeks Warwick and Clarence were in London, while Edward and his other brother Richard, Duke of Gloucester, were desperately trying to raise an army in the Low Countries to oust the invaders. The dire situation now meant that it was unsafe for the queen to remain even in the security of the Tower. On 4 October she took to the Thames in secret and travelled by barge, under the cover of darkness, upstream to Westminster Abbey, where she would seek sanctuary from Warwick and the frenzied mobs that supported him – and where she would give birth. Warwick and Clarence took control of the Tower two days later.

In the Middle Ages every church in England granted a general right of sanctuary to felons, who were entitled to receive protection from arrest for forty days within its walls. When their time was up they had to leave the kingdom and agree not to return, or face arrest. Special rights, over and above these, and granted by royal charter, applied to at least twenty-two churches, of which Westminster Abbey was one. These rights gave sanctuary dwellers immunity from capture and prosecution for life, even to those accused of high treason. Although sanctuaries were regarded as holy places to be treated with reverence, there were many instances of them being breached – most notoriously, by King Edward IV himself, who in 1471 entered Tewkesbury Abbey and dragged out the Lancastrians who had sought sanctuary within its walls. It comes as no surprise that the chronicler Dominic Mancini, an Italian monk who came to England in the retinue of the Bishop of Vienne and whose report entitled *The Occupation of the Throne of England by Richard III* is an important source of information for this period, wrote that 'sanctuaries are of little avail against the royal authority.'

Those seeking sanctuary at Westminster Abbey installed themselves not in the Abbey but in a dedicated building situated in the northwestern corner of the Abbey precincts, at the end of St Margaret's Churchyard. This sanctuary building dated from the time of Edward the Confessor, who had built the first stone church at Westminster. It was cruciform in layout, its stout oak door giving access to two chapels, an upstairs one for debtors and a lower one for common felons. Some writers have maintained that this is where Queen Elizabeth sought sanctuary in October 1470, and where her son Edward Plantagenet was born the following month. These include Agnes Strickland, the author of the seminal *Lives of the Queens of England*, published in several volumes during the course of the 1840s. In *Lives* Strickland describes Westminster's sanctuary as a 'gloomy building ... a massive structure, of sufficient strength to withstand a siege'. This sanctuary building was demolished – with great difficulty, as it was so massive – in 1750, and no trace of it remains. Middlesex Guildhall, a grand nineteenth-century edifice that is now home to the Supreme Court of the United Kingdom, stands today in its place; appropriately, it is surrounded by streets known as Little Sanctuary and Broad Sanctuary.

The right of sanctuary at Westminster was not limited to the sanctuary building. It also extended to the buildings surrounding the Abbey and its churchyard. Given this, it seems unlikely that the Queen of England would have chosen to give birth surrounded by common felons and debtors. Instead she probably lodged with the Abbot of Westminster, Thomas Millyng, in his house, Cheyneygates, situated beside the great west door of the Abbey. (Millyng is buried along with three other fifteenth-century abbots of Westminster in the Chapel of John the Baptist on the north side of Westminster Abbey, just across from its most sacred and oldest part, the Shrine of Edward the Confessor.) Cheyneygates itself still survives, or parts of it do. Today it takes the form of a rambling warren of hushed, carpeted corridors that link various public and private rooms spread over a number of levels, all of which cling limpet-like to the southwestern flanks of the Abbey. The Dean of Westminster – a successor to the medieval abbots – still lives in the private apartments in Cheyneygates, while the public rooms are given over to various abbey functions and meetings. Access is from an entrance in Dean's Yard, the great courtyard that adjoins the Abbey on its southern side (though none of Cheyneygates is open to the public). The buildings themselves range in age from the fourteenth to the twentieth century; the most recent as the result of extensive rebuilding after a direct hit from an incendiary bomb during the Second World War. Thankfully the most glorious room in Cheyneygates, known as the Jerusalem Chamber, where the Dean and Chapter conduct their meetings to this day, remained unscathed during the wartime inferno. In 1470 this was probably the main room placed at the disposal of Queen Elizabeth when she sought sanctuary; in addition she would have had use of Cheyneygates' Great Hall, a privy chamber, and the courtyard, where she could take fresh air. And it wasn't just Queen Elizabeth who sought sanctuary here; indeed she had quite a brood with her. This comprised her young daughters by King Edward IV – Elizabeth (born 1466), Mary (born the year after) and Cecily (born in 1469), along with her much older sons from her first marriage: Thomas, who was born in 1451 or 1455 (sources differ) and so was aged around 15 or 19, and Richard, who was

The Jerusalem Chamber is one of the oldest parts of the complex of buildings that make up Westminster Abbey. This was probably where Edward Plantagenet was born, in 1470. (*Photo courtesy Dean and Chapter of Westminster*)

later to play an important role in Edward Plantagenet's upbringing, and who was around 12 or 15 years old at the time.

The windows of the Jerusalem Chamber directly overlook the small courtyard by Westminster Abbey's great west door (the main entrance to the Abbey). Sandwiched as it is between the Abbey's gift shop and its western wall, the exterior of the Jerusalem Chamber attracts no interest from visitors. Inside, though, the room seems to breathe history, in a way that few other spaces can; the fireplace is Tudor and the panelling is Victorian, so both post-date the birth of Edward Plantagenet; but the high ceiling is original and dates from the time of Richard II (1367–99), whose crowned initials form part of its magnificently intricate design. Richard's successor, Henry IV, reputedly died in this room, some fourteen years after Richard was deposed; Henry's successor Henry V was then declared king in this same room (which is why busts of these monarchs are set against one wall). And on the night of 1 / 2 November 1470, Elizabeth Woodville was, according to the Burgundian chronicler Philippe de Commines, 'delivered of a son, in very poor estate', probably under this self-same ceiling. The anonymous author of the so-called Second Continuation of the Croyland Chronicle – a text written at the great abbey of Crowland in Lincolnshire in around April 1486, whose author was probably John Russell, Bishop of Lincoln and Lord Chancellor under Richard III – puts a more positive slant on the birth. 'From this circumstance derived some hope and consolation for such persons as remained faithful in their allegiance to Edward,' the chronicle states. As the baby boy took his first breath, King Henry VI, now rescued from the Tower and re-installed on the throne from which he had been deposed in 1461, had been king of England for just a day or so, placed there by Clarence and Warwick and the Lancastrian rebels fighting the infant's Yorkist father.

Though the new king was firmly on the 'other side', Henry VI's royal council nonetheless allocated funds for the royal birth taking place in its midst. Elizabeth Greystoke, Lady Scrope, was paid £20 to assist at the birth, during which she worked alongside Marjory (or Margaret) Cobb, the sanctuary midwife. The new arrival – named Edward, after his father – was baptised in Cheyneygates without any pomp or ceremony. Abbot Millyng and his Prior, John Esteney, were named the boy's godfathers, while Lady Scrope and Elizabeth's sister, Catherine, Duchess of Buckingham, were named his godmothers. Records show that in the days and weeks that followed, a butcher named John Gould kept the abbot's guests supplied with beef and mutton, while a fishmonger provided victuals for Fridays and fast days. The queen's Italian physician, Dr Dominic de Sirego, was also a regular visitor. So the queen was comfortably looked after; she was certainly in a better position than the debtors and criminals in the sanctuary building, which would have been visible from the windows of the Jerusalem Chamber. Yet Elizabeth's position was perilous. The French chronicler Jean de Waurin remarked that she and her children were in 'the greatest jeopardy they ever stood' while according to *Historie of the Arrival of King Edward IV in England,* a chronicle of Edward's resumption of the throne that was probably written by one of his servants, the family spent the whole five months of their sanctuary 'in right great trouble, sorrow and heaviness … the security of [Elizabeth's] person rested solely on the great franchise of that holy place' (throughout this book, text originally written in late fifteenth century English has been modernized to reflect contemporary styles of grammatization and spelling). However, Elizabeth sustained her ordeal 'with all manner of patience belonging to any creature, and as constantly as ever was seen by any person of such high estate to endure.'

Elizabeth's ordeal finally came to an end on 11 April 1471, when her husband King Edward marched triumphantly on London after invading England from the Low Countries the previous month. London quickly declared its loyalty to him and on the same day Henry VI was deposed and sent back to the Tower, a prisoner once again. This was Elizabeth's cue to leave sanctuary; along with her children she made the short journey from Cheyneygates to the adjoining Palace of Westminster, where she presented her husband the king with their new son. According to another chronicler, William Fleetwood, King Edward made his acquaintance with the boy 'to his heart's singular comfort and gladness', taking him into his arms and weeping as he did so.

Even as King Edward was joyously reunited with his wife and daughters, and was making the acquaintance of his new baby son for the first time, Warwick was still at large – and dangerous. The king allowed his family to spend their first night of freedom at Baynard's Castle, a mansion house on the banks of the Thames near St Paul's Cathedral that had become the London headquarters of the House of York during the wars; but after this, for their own safety, the queen and her family headed for the royal apartments in the Tower of London. They did not have to stay there long. Warwick's forces were at last defeated on April 14 at Barnet, just north of London, and the 'kingmaker' was killed in the battle. His defeat and death aroused the ire of Margaret of Anjou, the wife of the newly-deposed king Henry VI, who landed at Weymouth with a hastily-assembled force and made her way through the West Country, raising troops as she did so. But her support was limited; on May 4 her forces were defeated at Tewkesbury, and on the same night as the victorious Yorkists returned from London, her husband Henry was murdered in the Tower of London, probably whilst the royal family were still in residence there. It seems probable that Richard, Duke of Gloucester, the king's brother, was among the murderers, but whether he wielded the knife or merely acted as an observer has never been proved. With his enemies now fully vanquished, Edward rewarded Abbot Millyng, Mother Cobb and Dr Sirego for their vital assistance at his son's birth, and set about re-establishing his household in the Palace of Westminster.

The Westminster sanctuary again, in 1483

Yet even then Elizabeth was not finished with Cheyneygates. Some twelve years after her first stay she was forced to seek sanctuary at Westminster a second time, after Richard of Gloucester had taken her eldest son Edward into custody in advance of the boy's coronation as King of England. The machinations of Richard's plot against the Woodvilles – or, from the perspective of Richard's supporters, the Woodville's coup against Richard – will be examined in detail in a later chapter. Suffice it to say that on 1 May 1483, with 12-year-old Edward in Richard's hands, Elizabeth Woodville again entered the Abbey's sanctuary, desperate now to keep her younger son Richard, aged 9, from befalling the same fate. (Richard was known as Richard of Shrewsbury during his lifetime, and will be in this book too, to prevent confusion with his half-brother, Richard Grey, and his uncle Richard, Duke of Gloucester, later King Richard III.) According to Thomas More, in his biography of Richard III, Elizabeth was at this time 'in great flight and heaviness … bewailing her [older] child's ruin, and her own misfortune' as she entered sanctuary with young Richard and other members of her family. And no wonder; the political situation in England was one of confusion and uncertainty. (It appears that More wrote his biography of Richard III largely for his own intellectual amusement; some have claimed that his humanism and integrity would have made him an objective observer. However, others have accused him of unfairly blackening Richard's reputation for ever, as it was his biography that Shakespeare used to portray a king who, in the opening soliloquy of *Richard III*, admits that he is 'subtle, false and treacherous' and 'determined to prove [himself] a villain'. 'He was writing down in a Tudor England what someone had told him about events that happened in a Plantagenet England when he himself was five,' is how the policeman-narrator of Josephine Tey's crime novel *Daughter of Time* dismisses More and his biography. 'Sunday-paper accounts of hysterical scenes and wild accusations.')

Elizabeth's move to sanctuary came after she had failed to raise an army to wrest her son Edward from Richard of Gloucester's clutches. Thomas Millyng's successor John Esteney, who had held the position of Abbot of Westminster since 1474, and who was Edward's godfather, was her last hope. Elizabeth brought with her to sanctuary her five daughters (aged 2 to 17), the eldest of whom would have had some recollection of their time in sanctuary during the time of Edward's birth; also with her were her brother Lionel, Bishop of Salisbury, and her son Thomas Grey, now Marquess of Dorset, who would definitely have been old enough to recall his earlier stay in Cheyneygates. (Despite Richard of Gloucester's soldiers and guard dogs, the Marquess managed to escape sanctuary and head for France, later playing a role in Buckingham's rebellion against Richard; his grandson, the third Marquess of Dorset, was the father of Lady Jane Grey, the ill-fated 'nine day queen' of the Tudor era – another political *naïf* who came to grief at the hands of ambitious and vastly more experienced political power-players during a succession crisis to the throne.) With the future of the kingdom at stake, the queen and Dorset also brought some gold from the royal treasury from the Tower into sanctuary with them.

One of Elizabeth's first visitors at Cheyneygates was Archbishop Rotherham of York, whose official London residence was York Place, beside the Abbey. He was Lord Chancellor and held the Great Seal of England, which he brought to Queen Elizabeth, thus symbolising her continued power and position in the face of Richard's apparent coup. According to Thomas More, the archbishop 'found much heaviness and rumble, haste and business' surrounding Elizabeth and her family as her belongings – 'chests, coffers, packs, fardels [bundles], trusses, all on men's backs' – were brought into Cheyneygates. It is thought that some of the Abbey walls had to be broken down to get everything in – and it is also believed that her principal place of residence this time was not the set of rooms around the Jerusalem Chamber but the rooms in the southern part of Cheyneygates that clustered around the abbot's dining hall.

The Dining Hall of the former Abbot of Westminster, where Elizabeth Woodville sought sanctuary from Richard of Gloucester. (*Photo courtesy Dean and Chapter of Westminster*)

Today these buildings overlook Dean's Yard; the hall itself, which was constructed in 1376, still retains its original roof, and is in daily use as a dining hall by pupils at Westminster School, the prestigious public school whose buildings are scattered around the streets, courtyards and squares immediately south of the Abbey (which its pupils use for their morning assembly). These buildings, too, are what are known today as 'Cheyneygates'; over time this name (whose origins are obscure) seems to have been applied to different parts of the rambling buildings that abut the southwest of the Abbey and the northeast corner of Dean's Yard. In sanctuary here, wrote More, 'the Queen sat alone, all desolate and dismayed … the Archbishop comforted in the best manner he could, showing her he trusted the matter was nothing so sore as she took it for.' After passing her the seal, Archbishop Rotherham told her to be 'of good cheer,' according to More (inventing the dialogue, as he does throughout his book). 'For I assure you,' More has the archbishop tell Elizabeth, 'if they crown any king other than your son, whom they now have with them, we shall on the morrow crown his brother, whom you have here with you.' Later on Rotherham looked out from the window of his residence and saw the Thames was 'full of boats of the Duke of Gloucester's servants, watching that no man should go into sanctuary, nor none pass unsearched.' His actions were rash; Richard of Gloucester – still travelling towards London with the young king – quickly deprived Rotherham of his office of Lord Chancellor, though the Archbishop retained his seat on the royal council.

London was tense with rumour and speculation as news spread of the imminent arrival of Richard of Gloucester and the boy-king, Edward. According to Dominic Mancini there became 'current in the capital a sinister rumour that the Duke had brought his nephew not under his care, but into his power, so as to gain the crown for himself.' Mancini went on to observe that some members of the royal council recognised Gloucester's 'ambition and his cunning [and] always suspected where his enterprise would lead.' Crowds gathered and militias formed, some supporting Richard, others supporting Elizabeth. Over the ensuing weeks both sides held firm as the bloody politics of the royal council played out; young Edward was kept at a distance from it all (and from his mother) in the Tower of London, where – supposedly – he was preparing for his impending coronation. But Elizabeth remained fast in her Westminster sanctuary.

By 16 June Gloucester had had enough. On that day he made a personal appearance at Westminster, with 'a great multitude … armed with swords and staves', according to the Croyland chronicle. With Edward's coronation nearing, Richard wanted the boy's younger brother to join him in the Tower, so that they could be prepared together for the spectacle. But this meant wrenching young Richard of Shrewsbury away from his mother and the safety of the abbot's house. 'The sanctuary buildings at Westminster [were surrounded] so tightly with Richard of Gloucester's men-at-arms that they could have broken in at a word,' is how Emma Darwin portrays the situation in her novel *A Secret Alchemy*, which tells the story of the fate of the princes from the perspectives of Elizabeth Woodville and her brother Anthony, Earl Rivers, who was Edward Plantagenet's guardian. 'From every window we could see them, and they us,' she has Elizabeth observe. 'To break sanctuary is a terrible thing. But I could not be sure Richard of Gloucester would not give such a word.'

Another novel set during this time is *The Seventh Son*, a fictional and sympathetic account by Reay Tannahill of the life of Richard III. In the novel she dramatises the scene that follows, where Richard finally squares up to Elizabeth at Westminster. She informs him:

> I am perfectly at home here … I have every comfort, and it is pleasant to have a change of scene. There is much coming and going from the almshouses and the tenements and shops, while it amuses my little son very much to watch the hungry monks trying not to run through the cloister on the way to the refectory.

Westminster Abbey had been founded in around 960 as a monastery church, and in the late Middle Ages it was home to a community of around fifty Benedictine monks – hence young Richard's apparent enjoyment of their comings and goings (though Richard of Gloucester was not impressed, considering his nephew's interest in the monks to be a 'very juvenile amusement for a nine-year-old'). Gloucester then compelled Cardinal Thomas Bourchier, the elderly Archbishop of Canterbury, to persuade Elizabeth to release her son to him. According to the Croyland Chronicle, Bourchier entered 'the sanctuary in order to appeal to the good feelings of the queen and prompt her to allow her son to come forth and proceed to the Tower, that he might comfort the king his brother.' When Elizabeth expressed her doubts, Bourchier assured her that he would personally guarantee the boy's safety. Thomas More then takes up the story. 'The queen with these words stood a good while, in great thought', he wrote; but eventually she handed over her son – 'and therewith she kissed him, and blessed him, turned her back and wept and went her way, leaving the child weeping'. (Do the boys and girls of Westminster School know that a drama of this magnitude was once played out in the place where they eat their lunch?) More added that Elizabeth did not trust Richard, but nonetheless handed the boy over, guessing that if she did not, Richard might enter the sanctuary and take her son by force.

Two contrasting views of the events in the abbot's home on that day of tension and high drama can be found in the famous 1868 painting by John Zephaniah Bell, *Cardinal Bourchier Urges the Widow of Edward IV to let her Son out of Sanctuary*, and in the 1939 film *Tower of London*, a campish retelling of history starring Basil Rathbone as Richard of Gloucester. In Bell's painting Elizabeth, centre stage, keeps tight hold of Richard, who clings desperately to her skirts; the archbishop seems persuasive as Elizabeth's daughters look on. Was the boy literally pulled from his mother's arms? Or was there a calm but emotional parting, as Thomas More suggests? The makers of *Tower of London* assume the latter, depicting a highly charged but unforced parting between mother and son; the latter, sporting absurd blond locks (as in the famous painting by John Everett Millais, an extract from which is reproduced on the cover of this book) and dressed in a black tunic, seems positively keen on being reunited with his brother ('Give my love to him,' Richard's mother tells him as the boy is delivered into the kindly arms of Lord Hastings).

On leaving the abbot's home, young Richard was taken first to the Palace of Westminster, where according to Simon Stallworth (in a letter he wrote to the MP and highly respected soldier Sir William Stonor of 21 June, and still preserved in the collection of correspondence known as the Stonor letters) he was presented to Gloucester in the Palace's Great Hall. 'My Lord Protector received him at the Star Chamber door with many loving words,' Stallworth says (at the time the Great Hall was used for trials as well as feasts and ceremonial occasions; Stallworth himself was a secretary to Bishop John Russell, later Richard III's Lord Chancellor, and his preserved letters form a major source of information on this period). Then Gloucester's henchman Lord Howard, along with Archbishop Bourchier, conducted Richard of Shrewsbury by boat downstream along the Thames to the Tower of London, where the boy joined his older brother.

Edward's coronation, of course, was not to be. Elizabeth's marriage was declared invalid, rendering her sons illegitimate and therefore barred from the throne; and Richard of Gloucester was duly crowned the following month. Elizabeth Woodville – no longer England's queen – remained in sanctuary for another eight months, until March 1484, when she reached an agreement with Richard that guaranteed her own safety and that of her daughters. The Croyland Chronicle recorded that she 'came to terms only after frequent entreaties as well as threats had been made use of'. A year later, after Richard's defeat at Bosworth, the Abbey witnessed the coronation of the victorious Henry VII and, a few weeks later, his marriage to Elizabeth of York, Elizabeth's daughter and the princes' older sister. By then rumours had been circulating for months that Elizabeth Woodville's sons had died in the Tower. Some scholars have suggested that Elizabeth's willingness to have her daughter married to Henry was a sign that she knew that her sons were dead, otherwise why should she champion Henry VII as king, when her own sons had a much more valid claim to the throne? Others have turned this theory on its head, arguing that the boys were still alive when Henry acceded the throne, and Elizabeth's assent to his marriage to her daughter was part of a secret agreement to spirit them abroad to assume new identities. Elizabeth too had a new identity to forge for herself, in a way. On 10 July 1486 she took out a forty-year lease on Cheyneygates, seemingly intent on making this place of sanctuary her permanent home. But her plans were stymied the following February when parliament forfeited her estates, though granted her a pension of 400 marks per annum by some way of compensation. With this Elizabeth retired to Bermondsey Abbey, which lay across the Thames from the Tower of London. This eleventh-century monastery had long had royal connections but it was demolished after the dissolution (the scant remains of the south-western tower of the abbey church can be seen today below the glass floor of a restaurant at 11 Bermondsey Square). 'Sometimes [I] do nothing but sit at my window [in the abbey] and look over the rooftops to the river and beyond it the Tower,' Emma Darwin has Elizabeth lament in *A Secret Alchemy*. 'I know not if it is my sons' grave, but it is all the grave I can imagine'. She died in 1492 and was buried beside her husband Edward IV in St George's Chapel, Windsor – where a permanent reminder of her eldest son's brief rule can be seen in the form of a panel painting on the Bishop Oliver King Chantry Screen, which depicts a crown hovering above Edward Plantagenet's head, a motif to indicate that he was never crowned.

Edward and Richard Plantagenet at the Palace of Westminster

It is thought that Thorney Island, the creek-ridden islet beside the Thames that in the Middle Ages became the heart of English government, was first used as a site for a royal residence by King Canute (1016–1035). At the start of his reign the adjacent monastery and abbey had been in existence for around fifty years. Later in the same century Edward the Confessor either extended Canute's original palace, or knocked it down and started again; it's impossible to say which, but it's clear that by the 1050s the Confessor's new stone palace and his equally new abbey were rising together on this island, side-by-side. In the decades and centuries that followed, the palace became the principal residence of English monarchs – and the meeting place of their parliaments, including Simon de Montfort's parliament of 1295, which was the first to include representatives from each English town. In 1512, three years into the reign of Henry VIII, a devastating fire engulfed the palace, and Henry built its replacement on a new site close by at Whitehall, leaving what was left of the old palace to be used by parliament and law courts. In 1834 these buildings too were destroyed by fire – except the palace's Great Hall, now known as Westminster Hall, which today sits in the shadow of the familiar Victorian-Gothic Houses of Parliament; still sometimes known as the Palace of Westminster, these buildings arose from the ashes of the former medieval palace and were largely complete by 1850.

Between 1470 and 1483 the Palace of Westminster was the London home of Princes Edward and Richard and their parents, the king and queen. The Croyland Chronicle describes the Palace of Westminster during this time as 'a royal court such as befitted a mighty Kingdom, filled with riches and men from almost every nation, and surpassing all else within, the handsome and most delightful children born of the marriage ... to Queen Elizabeth'. Prince Edward's first household was established here when he was still an infant, soon after the political stability brought by the death of his father's foe, Warwick the Kingmaker. One of the first appointments to his household was a wet-nurse, since Queen Elizabeth, as was the practice of aristocratic women in the Middle Ages, did not breastfeed her own children. This position was held by Mrs Avice Wells, who on 12 November 1472 was granted an annual supply of red Gascon wine from the Port of London – which might have been a leaving present to mark the end of her service. Another key member of young Edward's household was Elizabeth Darcy, Lady Mistress of the Prince of Wales' Nursery, who had held the same position for the boy's older sisters, Elizabeth, Mary and Cecily. The most important appointment, however, was that of Sir Thomas Vaughan, who was appointed Edward's Chamberlain, and was given the responsibility of carrying the infant prince in his arms during ceremonial occasions. At the time of his appointment Vaughan was already the treasurer of the king's own chamber and a squire of the body (a personal attendant to the monarch) – among a string of other offices that he held. A formal patent of 12 January 1474 indicated that Prince Edward was so,

> young and tender in age that he cannot yet guide nor direct himself as it appertains to his high estate and dignity … [he needs] to have about him a true, witty, expert, loving and diligent chamberlain, as well for the surety and safeguard of his person as for hourly attendance and assistance in counsel and other matters that concern his honour and profit.

Vaughan became close to his young charge as he guided him towards boyhood, and had a house built for himself within the precincts of Westminster Abbey, where the prince would stay when he was in London. In 1483 Vaughan was one of the members of Edward's household who was taken into custody by Richard of Gloucester as Edward travelled to London for his coronation; he was executed at Pontefract Castle and lies buried in the Chapel of St John the Baptist in Westminster Abbey, with Thomas Millyng and the other fifteenth-century Westminster abbots. The inscription on his tomb simply reads 'Thomas Vaughan, Treasurer to Edward IV'.

Since the days of Edward of Caernarvon, later King Edward II (1307–27), the eldest sons of reigning monarchs had been created

Prince of Wales, and this honour was duly conferred on Prince Edward on 3 July 1471, when he was 8 months old. A Prince of Wales needs to be suitably attired, and it seems that Edward indeed was – and from a very young age. A surviving account record (held in the Public Records Office at Kew) shows that in late 1472 clothing was delivered for the 1-year-old prince that included five doublets priced 6*s* 8*d*, two of purple or black velvet and three of satin; five long gowns priced 6*s* 8*d*, three being satin – purple, black and green – and the others of black velvet; two bonnets, priced 2*s*, one of purple velvet lined with green satin and the other of black velvet lined with black satin; and a sixth long gown of cloth of gold on damask, priced £1. (Later wardrobe accounts record that the prince was dressed in a dazzling white outfit of cloth-of-gold at a gathering at the Palace at Christmas 1482, when he was 12 years old; the French chronicler Jean de Waurin wrote of this Christmas court – considered by scholars to be the first Renaissance court in England, in fact – as being 'worthy of a leading Kingdom, full of riches and men from every nation'.) In 1475 the queen was granted £2,200 per annum for the maintenance of Edward during the times he was at court. In the same year, on 12 May, when he was nearly 5 years old, Prince Edward made a state entry into London (on his return from Ludlow) and was knighted at the Palace of Westminster by his father. Two years later, on 9 November 1477, Richard of Gloucester led the Duke of Buckingham and a number of other leading peers in rendering homage to the 7-year-old prince – 'on both his knees', according to the records of the Bluemantle Pursuivant (a senior official in the College of Arms), now held in the British Library: 'putting his hands between the prince's hands, [Gloucester] did him homage for such lands as he had of him and so kissed him.' In response, the prince thanked 'his said uncle that it liked him to do it so humbly'. It is one of the few recorded speeches that Prince Edward made in his short lifetime.

What sort of boy was this, being brought up in castles and palaces, on whom so much expense and attention was lavished – and who, on occasions, was clearly treated with near god-like reverence by those around him? John Russell, Bishop of Lincoln (who might also have been the author of the Croyland Chronicle) wrote of Edward's 'virtuous disposition, gentle wit and ripe understanding, far passing the nature of his youth,' while Dominic Mancini commented that:

in word and deed he gave so many proofs of his liberal education, of polite, nay, rather scholarly attainments far beyond his age…. He had such dignity in his whole person, and in his face such charm that however much the might gaze, he never wearied the eyes of his beholders.

These and other similar comments were made when Edward was in London on one of his visits, and were based on the prince's bearing during formal and sometimes public occasions, mostly held at the Palace of Westminster. In private his manner and demeanour might have been different, revealing the genuine young boy behind the mask created by a rigourous upbringing – though as will be discussed in a later chapter, he does seem to have been genuinely gifted as regards learning and scholarship.

Fiction writers have had a field day conjuring a genuine character out of these contemporary portraits. In *The White Queen* Philippa Gregory describes Prince Edward, then 6 years old, as 'a straight-standing, handsome, fair-headed boy with a quickness of understanding … and the promise of good looks and charm that is all his father's', as the royal family gather at the Palace of Westminster to celebrate Christmas in 1476. In Josephine Tey's *Daughter of Time* Edward and his brother are shown to have 'all the character and good looks of their combined ancestry'. Yet later on in the novel one of the policeman's bedside visitors observes that Edward was probably 'a quite intolerable young man, actually, and long overdue for pushing into the pit. Perhaps [he] was just sitting up and begging to be quietly put down.' Vanora Bennett, in her novel *The Portrait of an Unknown Woman*, which recounts the love affair between an adopted daughter of Sir Thomas More and a grown-up Richard of Shrewsbury (who has been given a new identity after surviving imprisonment in the Tower), portrays a different boy entirely. She describes Edward as 'a quiet child, small and thin for his age,' in contrast to the 'terrifying blond tornado' of his legendarily rapacious, high-living father the king.

In complete contrast is the portrayal of Edward in Terrence Morgan's novel *The Master of Bruges*. Morgan plays on the fact that Edward was receiving intensive medical treatment during his time in the Tower, which has led some to suppose that he was ill for much of his life. He is 'a sickly youth', Morgan writes of the prince in a scene set in December 1482, when Edward was just a month past his twelfth birthday, 'with some deformity of the lower jaw which caused him to slobber saliva, pus and blood, [giving] his face a lopsided look as well as making him shy of being seen.' Later – when Edward is king – his condition worsens, leading to,

> a constant flow of a mixture of blood and saliva [dribbling] from the corner of his mouth, where there was wadding which Doctor Argentine, [his] physician, changed every hour. There was a foul stench around the unfortunate monarch emanating from the mess of corruption in his jaw … the missing teeth and constant bleeding gave his face a curious look, and he was forced to wipe his mouth two or three times a minute.

A pious, timid boy, Terrence Morgan's Edward is convinced that God is punishing him for 'some slight he was unaware of', while Doctor Argentine had diagnosed 'necrosis', the gradual death of skin tissues, and was treating his young patient's distressing condition with herbs and ointments.

In contrast to Edward, whose permanent household from the age of 3 was on the Welsh borders and who travelled extensively around Southeast England and the Midlands, Richard of Shrewsbury's upbringing seems to have mainly confined him to London, and specifically to the Palace of Westminster. One of his first public appearances came on 28 May 1474, when he was just shy of his first birthday. On this occasion a grand ceremony concluded by a tournament was staged to celebrate his creation as Duke of York (thus beginning the tradition, which continues to this day, of the second born son of the monarch being given this title). Parliament adjourned to allow MPs to attend the event – though a 1923 biography of Edward IV maintains that there were comments about excessive entry fees to the tournament field. The following year, on 18 April, both princes were knighted at Westminster on the eve of their father's invasion of France, along with their older step brothers, Thomas and Richard Grey. As for young Richard's life at the palace, it is known that he had his own apartments, heated – according to Edward IV's household ordinances from 1478 – by 'eight faggots and four bundles of coal'; it also seems that he had his own officials (and seal) – though the dominant figure in his life, particularly at first, would have been his mother. Little is recorded by the chroniclers as to Richard's looks and personality (though the French chronicler Jean Molinet says he was 'joyous and witty, nimble, and ever ready for dances and games') – giving fiction writers a blanker canvas to play with in contrast to his older brother, who (given his status as a future king) had much more written about him. The novelist Reay Tannahill has Richard attending a 'grand official banquet' at the Palace of Westminster to celebrate his older brother's seventh birthday, where Richard, aged 4¼, 'was perched on a bed-seat beside the cloth of state, sitting up stiffly to receive homage from members of the court after they had paid homage to his brother'. In *The Master of Bruges* Terence Morgan describes a slightly older Richard as a young boy with 'fair colouring and good looks, very tall for his age and full of boyish fun' who took 'great delight in mixing paints' for the Flemish artist who is the novel's narrator, before 'diligently applying it to the backgrounds' – though the artist repaints the backgrounds to his own satisfaction once the enthusiastic boy has departed his studio for the day.

Many of the public events that Edward and Richard Plantagenet attended at the Palace of Westminster would have taken place in what is now

Westminster Hall, built in the late eleventh century, is one of the few remaining parts of the medieval Palace of Westminster. Both princes would have made public appearances here. (*Source, John Lubbock - Wikimedia Commons*)

Another view of Westminster Hall. (*Source, John Lubbock - Wikimedia Commons*)

Westminster Hall. This was (and is today) famed for its enormous size – when William Rufus built it in the 1090s, it was possibly the largest such hall in Europe – and its astonishing hammer-beam ceiling, commissioned in 1393 by Richard II. In the Middle Ages the hall would have been a venue for coronation feasts, and the princes would have attended many celebratory banquets and other ceremonial events here (including, as will be described later, the wedding feast that celebrated the 'marriage' of Richard of Shrewsbury and Anne Mowbray); and it was in this hall – as previously noted – that Richard of Shrewsbury was presented to his uncle Richard of Gloucester after his removal from sanctuary, and just before joining his older brother in the Tower of London. Today, Westminster Hall is a space rich in historical resonance, though it struggles to find a purpose other than being a mightily imposing and ancient space. Plaques on the floor commemorate the fact that this was where Kings George V and VI, Queen Elizabeth the Queen mother and Winston Churchill were laid in state following their deaths; other plaques record that this is where Thomas More and Charles I were tried and condemned to death. Access to the Hall is restricted – it's occasionally used for exhibitions, when public access is fairly straightforward, but most of the time it can only be seen by those who have organised a tour of the Houses of Parliament, which must be arranged well in advance. All of this is a shame, as, like the Jerusalem Chamber, Westminster Hall is one of the most astonishing medieval buildings in central London – and one of the few that has direct links with the Princes in the Tower.

St Stephen's Chapel

At the heart of the Palace of Westminster was St Stephen's Chapel, built in the latter part of the thirteenth century as a place of worship for the monarch and his immediate family. It survived the great inferno of Henry VIII's era and in Tudor times it served as the debating chamber of the House of Commons. However it too went up in flames in 1834, during the next great fire, leaving only the chapel's crypt, known as the Chapel of St Mary Undercroft, to survive into the modern era – the only remaining relic, alongside Westminster Hall, of the great palace of medieval English kings. (Today the children of peers have a right to use the Chapel of St Mary Undercroft as a wedding venue – though it's not open to the public.) In 2013 the body of Margaret Thatcher was laid there in state the day before her funeral; over five centuries previously, the body of King Edward IV had lain in state in the upper chapel for a week, prior to it being taken to Windsor for burial.

Two royal weddings are recorded as having been held in St Stephen's Chapel. The first was the marriage in 1382 of King Richard II to Anne of Bohemia. The second, in 1478, was utterly extraordinary, to modern eyes: it was the marriage of Richard of Shrewsbury, then aged just 4, to his bride, Ann Mowbray, who was barely a year older than him.

The wedding came at a time when Edward IV was busy marrying off his children. In 1476, having betrothed his daughter Elizabeth to the French Dauphin (she eventually married King Henry VII), the king opened negotiations with Ferdinand and Isabella, joint monarchs of a newly united Spain, regarding a possible marriage between his 6-year-old son Edward and their daughter Isabella. These dragged on for two years until 1478, when Isabella gave birth to a boy, Juan, which meant that the Infanta was now less likely to inherit the Spanish throne. Edward's interest waned and he turned then to the daughter of the Duke of Milan as a possible marriage candidate for his growing son. But the duke's widow, Bona of Savoy, whom

Warwick the Kingmaker had tried to marry off to Edward himself ten years previously, opposed the match. So Edward moved onto the next candidate, Anne of Brittany, and here met with more success; her father Duke Francis II ratified her betrothal to Prince Edward on 23 June 1481, when Edward was approaching his eleventh birthday and Anne was just 4. It was agreed that she would marry Edward when she reached the age of 12 and would travel to Britain with a dowry of 100,000 crowns, half of which was payable at the wedding, that their first son would inherit England, and the second Brittany. If Anne died, Edward was to marry her sister; such were Prince Edward's expectations when he became king less than two years later.

By that time the king's second son, Richard of Shrewsbury, had long been accounted for in terms of a bride, and unlike his older brother, who had never met his intended wife, Richard had not only undergone a marriage ceremony with his 'wife', he had also had the experience of living under the same roof as her. The 4-year-old Anne Mowbray was Duchess of Norfolk in her own right, a title she had held since she was 2, when her father John Mowbray, the last of the Mowbray Dukes of Norfolk, died in January of 1476. The Mowbrays were one of the wealthiest families in late medieval England, with extensive estates in East Anglia, the East Midlands, Sussex and Surrey; King Edward made sure that his son would inherit the Mowbray fortune even if Anne died first. Formal dispensation was needed from the Pope for the marriage to take place, as the 'couple' were related – Richard's grandmother being the sister of Anne's great-grandmother. With dispensation duly granted, the stage was set on 15 January 1478 for the actual wedding at St Stephen's Chapel – a detailed description of which is preserved in Oxford's Ashmolean Museum; possibly written by a herald (that is, an officer-of-arms employed by the sovereign to participate in and arrange important ceremonial events), the account provides a vivid commentary on the proceedings.

On the evening before the wedding Anne was escorted by Earl Rivers, the queen's brother and guardian to Edward Plantagenet, and the Earl of Lincoln, Edward IV's nephew, into the king's great chamber in the Palace of Westminster, where she dined with the royal family and members of the nobility and gentry. After a night spent at the palace she was escorted, on her wedding morning, to St Stephen's Chapel, which had been brightly painted and gilded more than a century earlier by Edward III, and was now adorned for this occasion with rich hangings of royal blue, and golden fleurs-de-lis, the symbol of English royalty. The whole of the extended royal family was already there in attendance, including 7-year-old Edward, who had travelled from Ludlow for his younger brother's grand occasion, and also Cecily, Duchess of York, who was both the grandmother of the groom and the great-great aunt of the bride. At the entrance to the chapel Bishop Goldwell of Norwich stood waiting to receive the bride, but as the procession approached him, it was halted by Dr Coke, who ceremonially objected to the marriage on the grounds that the couple were too closely related – whereupon Dr Gunthorpe, Dean of the Chapel Royal, produced and read out the dispensation from the Pope. 'Thereupon,' the account reads, 'the said Bishop of Norwich proceeded to the marriage, and asked who should give the Princess to the church and to him; and the King gave her, and so proceeded to the high altar to mass'. It might well be that Anne spent the whole ceremony carried in the arms of an attendant, except for the part when Richard placed a ring on her tiny finger (in the 1939 film *Tower of London* Anne stands throughout the ceremony, gently bossing around her young bridegroom while cohorts of choir boys with medieval bowl cut hairstyles croon away in the background).

After the ceremony Richard of Gloucester and the Duke of Buckingham conducted the princess out of the chapel to the wedding banquet in the palace's Great Hall, where according to the eyewitness account, 'the abundance of the noble people was so innumerable'. The account even has details of the seating plan, and the minstrels that provided accompaniment after the second course. In *The White Queen* Philippa Gregory describes how at the feast 'the four-year-old prince and the little girl are lifted onto the table … in their beautiful miniature clothes, and they hold hands like a pair of little dolls.' Reay Tannahill also describes the wedding feast in her novel *The Seventh Son*.

> The gold and jewels were blinding, the furs and velvets suffocating, the fires and candles sweltering, and the conversation clamorous. Anne [Richard of Gloucester's wife] could have wept for the little bride and groom, who looked pale and terrified. Would they live long enough, she wondered, for their marriage to be confirmed and consummated?

But even then the festivities were not over. Three days later the king created twenty-four new Knights of the Bath, and four days after that a great tournament was held at Westminster, organised by Earl Rivers, with jousting and other displays. Princess Anne presided, and awarded prizes to victors that comprised jewel-like golden letters set with diamonds – the letters in question being A, E and M; A standing for Anne, M standing for Mowbray, and E standing for Edward – father or son – but also for the queen, the King's eldest daughter and the bride's mother, all of whom were named Elizabeth. At the ceremony Richard of Shrewsbury was invested with several titles including Duke of Norfolk, Earl of Nottingham, Earl Warenne, Earl Marshal, and Lords Seagrave, Mowbray and Gower.

Westminster Abbey: Amongst the Tombs in Henry VII's Lady Chapel

In May 1479 Richard of Shrewsbury added Lord Lieutenant of Ireland to his growing list of titles. It is probable that by now his mother was raising him, his sisters and his 'wife' together in the same household in a dedicated wing of the Palace of Westminster. However, tragedy struck on 19 November 1481, three weeks before Anne's ninth birthday: the little girl died, of unknown causes, leaving Richard a widower at the age of just 8. She was buried in Westminster Abbey's Chapel of St Erasmus, Elizabeth Woodville's own foundation, with one biographer of Edward IV maintaining that the cost of the funeral ($£215$ 16s 10d) was nearly as much as the wedding itself. Just over twenty years later the Erasmus chapel was demolished to make way for Henry VII's magnificent new Lady Chapel, which was built as an eastern extension to the abbey. Anne's coffin was exhumed during the rebuilding and was reburied in the Abbey of the Minoresses of St Clare without Aldgate, a nunnery situated around 400 metres north of the Tower of London. This foundation survived until its dissolution in 1539; thereafter the ruins slowly crumbled away until a fire in 1797 did for what was left. By then another church, Holy Trinity, had risen on this site but it too bit the dust during the Second World War, when a bomb reduced it to rubble. Today nothing remains of either church; the location is marked by a small parking lot on St Clare Street, which leads off a street simply named Minories – both names, of course, recalling the medieval foundation that once stood here.

It took nearly twenty years for the rubble of Holy Trinity Church to be cleared. During the clearance, on 11 December 1964, workmen discovered a lead-lined coffin in a vault beneath the church. It was at first taken to a police station in nearby Leman street; after it was ascertained that the coffin was medieval in origin, meaning that the remains inside would be of no interest to the Coroner, it was transferred to the Museum of London, after an eagle-eyed policeman noticed a Latin inscription on the coffin lid and deduced that the incumbent was of high station. A Latin scholar later deciphered the whole text, and reached the conclusion that this was the coffin of Anne Mowbray. The discovery of the coffin caused something of a stir, particularly among the descendants of Anne Mowbray's family, who trace their ancestry back to a brother of Geoffrey de Mowbray, Bishop of Coutances and an adviser to William the Conqueror. (The current Lord Mowbray is Edward Stourton, 27th Baron Mowbray, a hereditary peer and a cousin of the prominent writer and broadcaster of the same name.) Dr Lawrence Tanner, who was Librarian and Keeper of Muniments in Westminster Abbey and who had, in the 1930s, examined the bones that were purportedly those of the Princes in the Tower, was tasked with examining the remains. 'I saw the body a few days after the coffin had been opened and a very distressing sight it was,' he later recalled. But Anne's 'masses of brown hair' were still intact and her teeth were well preserved enough for a special examination to be made of them. Later her coffin was laid in state in the Jerusalem Chamber in Cheyneygates, prior to its formal interment in Henry VII's Lady Chapel in the presence of Lord and Lady Mowbray, the Home Secretary and the Director of the Museum of London.

Today Henry VII's magnificent Lady Chapel is one of the most evocative spaces within Westminster Abbey. It is hung with resplendent banners of the Knights of the Bath, and is overlooked by some wonderfully intricate fan vaulting. Originally intended as a burial place for Henry VI, whom Henry wanted to have canonised, the chapel was finally finished and dedicated in 1512, three years after Henry's death. It's essentially an eastern extension to the main body of the Abbey, itself constructed between 1245 and 1272 to replace Edward the Confessor's original church (though work on the abbey's nave was still ongoing even in Henry VII's day). But the Lady Chapel is almost a church in its own right; a Renaissance jewel adjoining a Gothic behemoth, and the final flowering of pre-Reformation art at Westminster before the monastery was dissolved by Henry VIII in 1540. Henry VII himself, and his wife Elizabeth of York, are buried in an ornate marble and gilt bronze tomb (surrounded by an elaborate bronze screen) at the chapel's eastern end, along with King James I. Anne Mowbray is buried in a small side chapel in roughly the same position

Henry VII's Lady Chapel is one of the most evocative spaces within Westminster Abbey. The tomb of Henry VII and his wife Elizabeth, the princes' sister, is at the far end. The princes' tomb is located in an aisle behind the left wall.

as the coffin had originally been interred in the Chapel of St Erasmus in 1481. Today a chamber organ covers the marker that indicates her grave, which sits among those of other aristocratic children from later centuries. Given this, it is not surprising that the side chapel commemorating

Anne Mowbray, who underwent a marriage ceremony with Richard of Shrewsbury when both were still small children, is buried in this side-chapel in Westminster Abbey; her grave marker is covered by a small chamber organ.

those who died in the Battle of Britain, as well as a marker indicating Oliver Cromwell's original place of burial – not to mention the tomb of Henry VII and Anne's sister-in-law, Elizabeth of York – are rather more successful at drawing the eye in this part of the Abbey.

Westminster Abbey: the Tomb of the Princes

The aisles on either side of Henry VII's Lady Chapel are crammed with tombs. In the south aisle lies Henry's mother, Margaret Beaufort, the Countess of Richmond. She was one of the most formidable women of the Tudor era, and both fiction writers and historians – of an unorthodox mindset – have suggested that it was she who had ordered the murder of the Princes in the Tower, to further her son's ambitions for the throne. Henry's grand-daughter Margaret Lennox and his great-grand-daughter Mary Queen of Scots, whose tomb is one of those in the Abbey that most draws the crowds, are also buried in the south aisle. In the north aisle – entered through a narrow stone arch – are Henry's grand-daughters Elizabeth I and Mary Tudor, half-sisters divided by religion in life but united in the Abbey in death. They are buried in an extravagant tomb covered by an ornate canopy and surrounded by an iron railing. Beyond the tomb of the half-sisters, at the far end of this aisle, is the reputed final resting place of the boys who were great uncles to Queens Mary and Elizabeth – Edward and Richard Plantagenet, the princes in the Tower.

The tomb of the princes in Innocents' Corner, situated at the end of an aisle that runs along the north side of Henry VII's Lady Chapel. The supposed remains of the princes are interred within a tomb of white marble.

30

Above: The tomb of the princes in Innocents' Corner, situated at the end of an aisle that runs along the north side of Henry VII's Lady Chapel. The princes' supposed remains lie within a tomb behind two infant daughters of King James I.

Right: Innocents' Corner, Westminster Abbey. The tomb of the princes was designed by Sir Christopher Wren. Within lies an urn containing the remains of two children dug up in the Tower of London in 1674.

Their tomb of creamy-white marble sits in a raised niche behind two fussy seventeenth century tombs where Maria and Sophia, two infant children of King James I, are interred. An effigy of Maria reclines atop her tomb, surrounded by cherubs, while Sophia has been afforded a plainer tomb, with a headstone of black and gold. There's a one-way system around Elizabeth and Mary's tomb (the aisles are narrow; keep left) and this assemblage of children's tombs gets barely a mention from the tour guides – 'this is innocents' corner', they say to their shuffling groups, who are more interested in the two Tudor queens than the melancholy sight of dead Plantagenet princes and equally dead Jacobean princesses (two boys, two girls: a pleasing symmetry, like the arrangement of the tombs themselves). The tomb of the princes dates from a few decades after the burial of James I's infant daughters. It was designed by Sir Christopher Wren, who held the position of Surveyor General of His Majesty's Works, and who had direct responsibility for the upkeep of the Abbey. On 18 February 1675 he was commissioned by royal warrant to arrange for the construction of 'a white marble coffin for the supposed bodies of ye two princes lately found in ye Tower of London'; the tomb was actually constructed by Joshua Marshall, Master Mason to King Charles II. Within the tomb is an urn containing bones discovered in the Tower of London in 1674 by workmen repairing a staircase, and assumed at the time to be those of the two Plantagenet princes. The formal interment in the Abbey took place in 1678, as recorded in a long Latin inscription on the tomb's exterior; translated, the inscription reads:

> Here lie interred the remains of Edward V, King of England, and Richard, Duke of York, whose long desired and much sought after bones, after over a hundred and ninety years, were found interred deep beneath the rubble of the stairs that led up to the Chapel of the White Tower [in the Tower of London], on the 17 of July in the Year of Our Lord 1674. Charles the Second, a most merciful prince, having compassion upon their hard fortune, performed the funeral rites of these unhappy princes among the tombs of their ancestors, in the year 1678.

At the time of their burial, these bones were accepted as being those of the princes by senior legal authorities – though what convinced them

32

The inscription on the tomb of the princes in Westminster Abbey.

about their authenticity is unclear. Since then, many have doubted that the remains of the children discovered in the Tower were those of the princes, and in the opening years of the twentieth century there was pressure to open the urn and examine the bones, to see whether recent advances in medical science could throw any new light on them. Westminster Abbey is a 'royal peculiar', and as such both the sovereign (George V) and the Home Secretary of the day had to give permission for the urn to be opened. Permission was eventually granted in 1933, when the contents of the urn were examined jointly by Dr Lawrence Tanner and by Professor William Wright, a dental surgeon who was Professor of Anatomy at the London Hospital Medical School. Tanner wrote an extensive report on what they found in the journal *Archaeologia* in 1934. Unfortunately, although Tanner was quite convinced that the bones were those of the princes, the forensic techniques used by him and Wright have since been questioned, and far from conclusively confirming who exactly was buried in the urn their report has simply muddied the situation, adding yet another layer of mystery, conjecture and supposition to the already murky fate of the princes.

Tanner and Wright concluded from their examination that all sorts of bones, including animal bones, had found their way into the urn. Mixed in with these were the incomplete remains of two children, the older 4ft 10in inches tall and, according to dental records, around 12 or 13 years old (which is commensurate with Edward Plantagenet's age and probable height at the time of the accession of Richard III) and the other a little shorter and younger, 4ft 6½in tall and aged between 9 and 11 (Richard of Shrewsbury was 10). Both skeletons suggested children of slender frame; but because the bones were pre-pubertal their gender could not be established. Wright concluded that the older child had been suffering from extensive chronic bone disease, probably osteomyelitis, which must have caused painful swelling of the lower gums; this might account for Edward having been under the care of Dr Argentine when he was in the Tower (and doubtless inspired Terrence Morgan to concoct his unflattering description of a continuously slobbering Edward in his novel *The Master of Bruges*). Wright argued that the structure of the bones indicated a familial link between the two skeletons, and claimed that a red mark on the facial bones of the elder child was a blood stain caused by the severing of blood vessels during suffocation. The evidence in the urn was, according to Wright, 'more conclusive than could, considering everything, reasonably have been expected'; in other words, he was pretty convinced that the bones were those of Richard and Edward Plantagenet, and that the boys had died some time in late 1483. The manner of their deaths remained hazy, and even if they had been murdered, there was of course no way of telling who was the murderer by examining the skeletons. The remains were reinterred after the examination but Wright and Tanner left extensive notes and photographs behind, which contemporary authorities have since examined, often reaching conclusions at odds with those original findings from 1933.

Arguments put forward by these sceptics cover a number of areas. Some argue that the larger set of bones are those of a child much older than 13; others suggest that Tanner and Wright were too familiar with Thomas More's now discredited account of the deaths and burial of the princes, and that the examination was not properly objective. Some authorities have even questioned whether the bones buried in the tomb were actually those discovered in the Tower, claiming that souvenir hunters might have got their hands on some of the remains in the four years between their unearthing and their burial in the Abbey. Indicative of the shoddy way in which the bones had been looked after in the 1670s, between their discovery in the Tower and their burial at Westminster Abbey, is that the celebrated antiquarian and collector Elias Ashmole had actually removed some of the bones and had placed them in his new foundation, the Ashmolean Museum in Oxford (although the bones were recorded in a catalogue, when the antiquarian Thomas Hearne asked to see them in 1728 he was told by the museum's then keeper, a Mr Whiteside, that they could not be found. In 1933 another search was made for these bones but once again they proved elusive). However it does seem that prior to their burial the bones were examined by a number of authorities. One was John Gibbon, Bluemantle Pursuivante (that is, a junior officer of arms), who wrote in the College of Arms' copy of *A Catalogue of the Kings of England* that 'I myself handled the bones especially the king's skull'. Curiously, Gibbon states that although the skull of the younger child had been broken during the digging, the skull of the older child was not damaged. Yet Professor Wright found both skulls to be damaged in his 1933 examination, which suggests that the original skull of the older child might have been swapped at some time for a substitute one.

At least one scholar, however, has agreed with Tanner and Wright's original findings. Dr Jean Ross, Senior Lecturer in Anatomy at Charing Cross Hospital Medical School, concluded that the rare bone formations evident in Anne's skull matched those in the two skulls from the Abbey tomb, suggesting a familial relationship between all three and making it seem likely that the bones were indeed those of the princes (Anne Mowbray was their third cousin). Of the two skulls from the Abbey, the older one displays a distinct absence of four teeth, namely the second premolars on both sides of the upper jaw and the wisdom teeth on both sides of the lower jaw. The younger skull also displays an absence of teeth – this time the deciduous last molar on the right hand side of the lower jaw. The skull of Anne Mowbray likewise has missing teeth and Dr Ross concluded that this could have been because of hypodontia – a hereditary condition where babies are born with teeth missing. However, Anne's hypodontia could have passed down to her through her mother's bloodline, which the boys didn't share, and when the remains of Richard III were examined after being disinterred from a car park in Leicester in 2012, it was shown that he did not suffer from the condition – making it unlikely that it was prevalent within the family.

In the 1950s huge strides were made in our understanding of how once living tissue such as human bone can be dated in terms of its age. This technique, known as radiocarbon dating, relies on the fact that carbon 14, absorbed by human bones during a person's lifetime, then decays at a known rate after the person's death. In the 1970s and 1980s the Richard III society made several unsuccessful attempts for the bones in the urn in Westminster Abbey to be re-examined using this dating technique. All were refused by the Abbey authorities. Such an examination would of course throw much clearer light on the age of the bones. Even better, if a DNA test was conducted on them, then the collected DNA could be compared with that collected from Richard III's bones in 2012 – and, if there was a match, it would prove pretty conclusively that the remains were those of the princes. Other tests could determine whether the bones are male or female (female bone tissue has a higher content of citrate salts than males) and might re-examine the red stain on one of the skulls, which Wright believed to be blood, though others have suggested is a stain from a rusty nail. Without these rigorous scientific tests, however, the ascribing of the remains buried in Westminster Abbey to Edward and Richard Plantagenet remains a somewhat shaky proposition, to say the least.

Chapter Two

Ludlow, Shrewsbury and the Marches

There is a panel on the Bayeux Tapestry that shows a Norman knight, recently arrived on the shores of England in 1066, watching over the construction of his new castle. 'This man orders a castle to be dug at Hastings,' the pennant above him reads, and sure enough, beside the victorious knight are men armed with picks and shovels, setting to work on the new fortification.

The Norman Conquest ushered in an extraordinary era of castle building in England. Most were motte-and-bailey affairs, timber fortifications atop an earthen mound; but within a few years castles built of stone were beginning to rise where these once stood, and many of them still stand today. Typically, the impetus behind the building of a castle was to quell one of the numerous rebellions that broke out against the rule of William the Conqueror. 'The Normans built castles far and wide throughout the land,' lamented the Anglo-Saxon Chronicle for 1067, 'oppressing the unhappy people'. These castles embodied in stone William's right to rule, fulfilling both military and political roles; but they also ensured the safety of key trade routes, protecting the economy of Norman England. Even more importantly, they revolutionised how England was governed – for William organised his new domain into castle-centred lordships, and the lord of each castle was a Norman knight place there by him to keep the peace and enforce the new order.

Two Norman fortifications played a vital role in the story of the princes in the Tower. The most prominent was the Tower of London, where the boys were imprisoned and quite possibly died; the history of this most famous of fortresses, and its role in their story, is told in chapter five of this book. This present chapter, however, looks at Ludlow Castle in the area known historically as the Welsh Marches – the notoriously lawless region either side of the English-Welsh border. By the late fifteenth century this castle had been rebuilt as a palatial residence for a prominent family that could trace its heritage back to the Norman knights who had been tasked with the foundation of the castle some four centuries previously. How this castle came to play a role in the life of Edward Plantagenet, who was raised here, is a complex story, but one that is worth telling, as the fact that the castle survives today (albeit in a ruinous state) means that it provides a tangible link with the princes' lives; that the castle sits within one of England's most beautiful and historic towns, where more links with Edward's life can be found, particularly in the parish church, makes apparent the need for a wider exploration of Ludlow itself.

Welcome to Arcadia

In 2009 the magazine *Country Life* ran a feature entitled 'The Grand Tour of Britain'. The piece celebrated the joys and wonders of Britain through a number of pithy 'top five' lists – the best pubs, towns, walks and so on – compiled by various luminaries. The broadcaster and writer Jeremy Paxman, of *Newsnight* and *University Challenge* fame, was asked to provide his 'top five views' – and at the top of his list came the view of Ludlow Castle from the banks of the River Teme. Of the town itself, he wondered with a sigh, 'has there ever been a visitor to Ludlow who hasn't wished they lived there?' – and he is not alone; accolades of this sort attach themselves easily to this Shropshire town, which is cradled by the hills of the Welsh borderlands. In an earlier edition of *Country Life* – published over sixty years before the one that carried Paxman's comments – the magazine's architecture editor Christopher Hussey had pronounced that Ludlow stood 'perhaps first among English towns ... the whole place is a national monument, or rather should be,' and gushed over its 'sheer visual beauty, coloured by romantic history and substantiated in richness of architectural sequence.' Today, the town's appeal remains strong; the 2018 edition of *The Rough Guide to England* describes Ludlow as one of the 'most picturesque' towns in the country, 'a gaggle of beautifully-preserved Georgian and black-and-white half-timbered buildings packed around a craggy stone castle, with rural Shropshire forming a drowsy backdrop.'

The best place to appreciate this Arcadian scene is along the banks of the River Teme, which cuts a broad, curving course through a wooded

Ludlow Castle from the banks of the River Teme.

gorge on the town's western fringes. Above the gorge, the redoubtable walls of the sturdy medieval castle seem to grow organically from the rocks. No wonder painters and romantics have been drawn to this vista; among the first was a little-known poet named Thomas Churchyard (1520–1604),

Painting of Ludlow Castle by an anoymous artist, published in 1812. (*Source, Wikimedia Commons*)

Ludlow Castle became a popular day out in the ninteenth century. This sketch is from an 1852 book by Thomas Wright on the history of the town. (*Source, Wikimedia Commons*)

who flourished in the late Elizabethan era after a busy career as a soldier, in which he saw action on various European battle fronts. In his long poem *The Worthiness of Wales* – to whom Queen Elizabeth herself was the dedicatee – Churchyard wrote of the same view from the banks of the Teme that visitors today can drink in, the castle standing 'right well and pleasant to the view/With sweet prospect'. Seen from this aspect, you would be forgiven for thinking that Ludlow Castle is set in deep countryside – perhaps that of A.E. Housman's 1896 verse cycle *A Shropshire Lad*, a poem which celebrates this part of England, with its 'blue remembered hills,' and has become the byword for a yearning, almost painful nostalgia; 'a land of lost content' that, like youth, can never be revisited. But while a vista of river and forest and gorge characterises the castle's western flank, the eastern side opens onto a prospect that is very different – a sizeable, elongated market square that forms the heart of the busy town of Ludlow. 'On every side [of the market square] fair houses are,' Thomas Churchyard observed in his poem, 'that makes a show to please both mind and eye'. Over four centuries later, Ludlow's market square (properly, the High Street) still presents an aesthetically pleasing jumble of buildings (though most date from Georgian times, and would not have been known to Churchyard). Beyond the square lies a tight cluster of narrow lanes that open up into intimate urban scenes, where courtyards are fringed by half-timbered buildings whose upper storeys overhang passing pedestrians, just like they do in illustrations in children's books of medieval life. There are individual shops – how many towns these days can claim a retailer proudly calling itself a 'draper' – and on the market square itself is the fine Castle Bookshop, where customers pass the time of day with the genial bookseller before finally getting round to seeing whether a particular book is in stock (and ordering it for collection in a few days, if it isn't). It was this facet of the town that most struck the American travel writer Bill Bryson when he swung this way in 1995. In his book *Notes from a Small Island* he mused that Ludlow was 'a charming and agreeable place ... it appeared to have everything you could want in a community – bookshops, cinema, some appealing-looking tearooms, a couple of family butchers ... all neatly arrayed and respectful of their surroundings.' He seems to have missed, though, the town's most eye-poppingly gorgeous urban vista. This comes in the form of Broad Street, which runs up the hillside from the churning river to one of the town's former gates; a lane on one side of the street is sunken below street level, picturesquely separating the front doors of cottages from the road. The antiquarian and topographer John Leland noted in his *Itineraries*, a six-volume account of the journeys he undertook through England between 1538 and 1543, that this was 'the fairest part of town', and the architecture critic Nikolaus Pevsner was similarly impressed; in his 1958 book *The Buildings of England: Shropshire* he named Broad Street 'one of the most memorable streets in England'.

Like the rest of the town, Broad Street is preserved with a quiet sense of local pride. It is emblematic of Ludlow's good fortune, which in historical and architectural terms, is two-fold. Firstly, the town enjoyed a prosperous past, based on the wool trade but also on the presence of the castle, a home for princes and kings who repaid the loyalty of the townsfolk by endowing their town handsomely; and secondly, Ludlow has been spared the despoliation and development that has blighted many similar towns in the nineteenth and twentieth centuries. The railway, when it came, kept its distance from the town centre – meaning that today's visitors who arrive by train have a short stroll to reach the market square – while all the modern accoutrements of twenty-first century living, such as out-of-town retail parks and modern housing developments, are kept firmly in the background. Visitors are something Ludlow is not short of; the mainstay of Ludlow's tourism scene are the day-trippers and the weekend-breakers, and on a fine bank holiday weekend the place is heaving (an amble round the castle; a walk along the river; a stroll up Broad Street; a look around the shops; coffee and a slice of Victoria sponge in a tea room). In fact it is increasingly difficult to experience the Sundays that Housman wrote about, 'When Ludlow streets are still / And Ludlow bells are calling / To farm and lane and mill'. Yet the place is not as busy as it could be. Ludlow is not on a major through-route by road or rail. The nearest motorway is over an hour's drive away. There are no direct trains to London (actually, there aren't even any direct trains to Birmingham, just thirty-five miles away); instead, trains rumble north and south along patience-testing routes that lead (eventually) to Manchester (via Shrewsbury) and South Wales (via Hereford). So is the place a rural backwater, or a paradigm for a modern kind of civilised living? It's hard to draw conclusions: the food writer Jonathan Meades, extolling Ludlow's culinary reputation, echoed Jeremy Paxman's sentiments in 2002 when he remarked that Ludlow was 'the only place in England other than London where I ever want to live.'

More than anything it's an abiding sense of history – real and palpable, not imagined or phoney – that pervades Ludlow; it is present in every Georgian façade, in every bit of rough stone in the castle, in every Tudor beam. Part of that history – a small part – comes from Ludlow being the place where Edward Plantagenet, the older of the two 'little princes in the Tower' (as leaflets available at the tourist board and castle would have it), was sent by his father to be raised. But Edward's presence here was emblematic of a larger royal role for Ludlow that lasted several centuries and which resulted in the town growing into one of the most important political centres in England. Sir Roy Strong, the art historian and broadcaster, defined the sense of history that seems to seep from Ludlow's every pore when he wrote that:

> The secret of Ludlow resides in the fact that … it was once a seat of government in Tudor and Stuart England. A sense of its own identity and importance has never quite left it…. This is a town which, although the tide of history has receded from it, still manages to preside magisterially over the countryside one glimpses at the end of every street.

The Tide of History

The tide of history that led to Ludlow being a place where a prince was raised may be 'out' now, but five centuries ago it was well and truly 'in', lapping at the walls of the town's market hall and crashing against the cliffs on which the castle stands. It's a laboured analogy, of course, Ludlow is over 70 miles from the sea – yet 10,000 years ago a large water body *was* surprisingly close at hand, though taking the form of a lake of glacial meltwater rather than the salty ocean. Such lakes covered much of Britain as the ice melted after the last Ice Age, when it was warm enough for much of that ice to turn into meltwater, but cold enough still for large ice dams to trap the water and form county-sized lakes. When those lakes rose, their water eventually spilled over the landscape to form torrents that are unimaginable today; in a number of places those torrents cut the surrounding topography to shreds, eroding deep gorges with steep sides that are now filled with winding rivers that flow within a grand landscape. The Teme, emptying one of those nearby lakes, cut one such gorge at

The River Teme, viewed from Ludlow Castle.

Ludlow, and still flows through it today, providing natural ramparts for the castle that overlooks its gorge. So when the Norman conquerors came looking for a suitable location hereabouts to build a defensive structure, they found one that had been created for them by nature.

A Norman knight named Walter de Lacy was the castle's founder. He was tasked with defending this area after an uprising against the Normans led by Edric the Wild in 1068–9; a timber castle was built almost immediately after this, and within twenty years work had begun on a more permanent stone structure. But what of the adjacent town? For all its age and prosperity, and the sense of history that pervades it, the origins of Ludlow are shrouded in a mist thicker than that which gathers in the gorge of the River Teme on cold, still winter mornings (and above which the castle rises like a ship at sea). At the time of the castle's construction this was border country, sparsely settled and subject to frequent raids and burnings, and local history societies are kept busy wondering which came first – the castle or the town. Whether or not settlers were already living on the future site of Ludlow town when Walter de Lacy set his stonemasons

Ludlow Castle from the air. The town's market square is visible at top right. (*Source, Gareth Thomas - Ludlow Castle*)

Ludlow Castle viewed from nearby Whitcliffe. (*Source, Ian Capper - Wikimedia Commons*)

to work, what *is* certain is that several castles already stood guard over this volatile region as Walter's castle began to rise above the Teme. These three Herefordshire castles (along with another one in Essex) were the only castles in England at the time of the Norman Conquest. They had been constructed by Ralph of Vexin, Edward the Confessor's French nephew, whom Edward had placed in charge of Hereford, and who imported the new architectural fad for castle-building from his native France. Walter de Lacy, who hailed from the tiny Normandy village of Lassy (Anglicised to Lacy), served William as a knight for a while before being tasked with laying the first stones of Ludlow Castle. But only a small amount of work had been completed when Walter died in 1085. His son Roger took the helm but was exiled to Normandy in 1096 after rebelling against William the Conqueror's successor, William Rufus, and the castle duly passed into the hands of Roger's brother Hugh, who completed the building work in the first two decades of the twelfth century.

Castles needed a workforce. They also tended to attract settlers; where could be a better place to live, in this troubled border country, than in the defensive shadow of a great fortress? This, then, was the probable origin of Ludlow town, whether or not there were clusters of farmsteads here before. By 1233 the town had acquired defensive walls, and by the end of the Middle Ages it had a population of around 2,500; wool merchants and local officials brushed shoulders in Ludlow's narrow streets, for by the time of Leland's visit this was a centre of politics as well as commerce. Ludlow's late medieval prosperity was the result of its development as a vital centre for the production of high quality cloth, which was sold as far away as London, Southampton and Bristol, and found its way into foreign markets via merchants from Genoa and Venice. Weavers, dyers and hosiers formed the town's social, religious, economic and political backbone; they lived in homes that they built for themselves along Broad Street and Mill Street, some of which still survive, and when they died, their families endowed chantries to their memory in St Laurence's Church. Centuries of royal patronage, emanating from the castle, paid dividends too, and ensured Ludlow's prosperity, sustaining the town as one of the most important commercial hubs of the Welsh Marches and the English Midlands.

Mortimer and Plantagenet: how Ludlow came into royal hands

The most vital role in the story of how Ludlow became a royal castle that was favoured by kings – and how it came to shelter Edward Plantagenet – was played by Edward's grandfather, Richard Plantagenet, the third Duke of York (1411–1460). A small, hard-featured man, haughty and arrogant in manner, Richard was a leading soldier and military administrator (it is said he was the Richard of York who 'gave battle in vain' in the famous mnemonic used for remembering the colours of the rainbow). Holding the earldoms of March and Ulster, Richard was the greatest landowner in England after the king, and Ludlow was his principal seat. He considered himself to be heir presumptive to the throne of England, and to emphasise his claim he adopted the surname 'Plantagenet' to highlight his descent from Geoffrey of Anjou, the French count who first took the name and whose son, Henry II, was the first Plantagenet king of England. Richard's ambitious streak, however, was drawn more from his being descended from Edward III through both parents: his paternal grandfather had been Edmund Langley, first Duke of York and the youngest son of Edward III, while through his mother, Anne Mortimer, he could trace his family line back to Lionel, Duke of Clarence, Edward III's third son. Through this lineage he considered himself a worthy claimant to the throne of England, and ridiculed the claim to the throne of Henry VI – who became king in 1422 (at the age of 9 months) when Richard was 11 years old – as being inferior to his own. Henry, Richard scoffed, was merely a descendant of Edward III's fifth son, while Richard's patrimony stretched back to one of Edward's older sons. On the basis of this claim was fought the war known at the time as the Cousins' War, and later as the Wars of the Roses. In the event, Richard was never to take the throne of England, but he sired two future kings, Edward IV and Richard III; he was grandfather to another, Edward V; and Henry VIII and the subsequent Tudors were all descended from him through his granddaughter, Elizabeth of York. Richard's dynastic achievement came about as a result of his ancestors making a series of judicious marriages and involving themselves in some audacious political manoevres that stretched back centuries.

Recognising that the Welsh borderlands were an area of considerable tension, William the Conqueror had appointed a number of his closest allies to leading positions there, where they established the 'Marches' as a buffer zone between England and Wales. One, of course, was Walter de Lacy, who founded Ludlow Castle. In theory – and certainly in Norman times – these Marcher lords were independent of the English crown, ruling mini-fiefdoms as if they were kings. But gradually that independence was hacked away, and through marriage and inheritance and the deliberate English settlement of new towns such as Ludlow, the Marches became inexorably tied to the English crown. Over the course of the thirteenth century the powerful Mortimer family – whose influence is recalled in the names of Marcher towns such as Mortimer's Cross and Cleobury Mortimer, and whose castle was at Wigmore, just 7 miles southwest of Ludlow – jostled themselves into pole position among all the Marcher lords. In 1301 the 14-year-old Roger Mortimer, scion of the family, married Joan de Geneville, the grand-daughter of Geoffrey de Geneville, the lord of Ludlow Castle, so bringing the castle into Mortimer hands. Roger made himself the first Earl of March and under his successors the earldom of March became a powerful semi-independent fiefdom, complete with its own seal, chancellor, receiver and records that were largely independent of parliament. Roger's domain incorporated parts of present-day Shropshire and Herefordshire on its eastern side, and stretched deep into present-day Wales in the west. As the earldom became established the Mortimers moved their principal seat from Wigmore (these days little more than a few spikey walls and stumpy towers in the middle of nowhere) to Ludlow, which was slightly further away from the Welsh border and so slightly safer from raids. But the Mortimer line came to an end in 1425, when Edmund Mortimer died of the plague at Trim Castle in Ireland. This is where Richard Plantagenet enters the scene; he was the son of Edmund Mortimer's sister, and therefore inherited the Earldom of March and, with it, Ludlow Castle. Just 13 years old at the time, Richard had spent much of his boyhood in Yorkshire, in the household of Ralph Neville, the Earl of Westmorland. Five years later, when he was 18, he abandoned the north, moving his political base to Ludlow, which was by then, to all intents and purposes, the 'capital' of his new Marcher earldom. Over the years that followed Richard got to know the Marches and the people who lived there well. This was his home turf, and when he had sons, he chose Ludlow as the place where two of them should be raised.

Those two sons were Edward, born in 1442, the future King Edward IV and the father of the princes, and Edmund, born a year later in 1443, who was destined to die with his father on the field of battle at the age of just 17. A letter written jointly by Edward and Edmund at Ludlow Castle in 1454, when the boys were 12 and 11 years old respectively, still survives. In it they wish their father well in his 'prevail against the intent and malice of your evil willers' and thanked him for his gift of 'our green gowns', requesting 'some fine bonnets' to complete the outfits. Just six years later Richard Plantagenet was dead and his son, by then 18, was raising an army at Ludlow. Edward defeated a Lancastrian force at Mortimer's Cross, 10 miles to the southwest, before marching on London to claim the crown, which he did with the help of the Earl of Warwick, known as the 'kingmaker'; he was duly crowned King of England on 4 March 1461.

Ludlow Castle in Norman and Plantagenet times

The people of Ludlow had proved themselves loyal to Edward's cause throughout his years of campaigning, and ten years after his coronation he was able to endow the town with the greatest royal patronage possible – that of being the place chosen by the King of England to raise his eldest son. Not only was Ludlow a place that Edward IV knew and loved from his own boyhood, but the traditional reputation of the Marches for lawlessness still prevailed. 'We must have more authority there',

Edward tells Elizabeth in Emma Darwin's novel *A Secret Alchemy*. 'No charter I can give to a council will have the power over men that a Prince of Wales does.' Darwin has Elizabeth acquiesce easily, knowing that in reaching his decision Edward 'was thinking again of his own youth, hunting and dancing and jousting with his brother Edmund among those round, dark Welsh green hills.'

So in the spring of 1473, King Edward, his wife Elizabeth and their infant son Edward, then a toddler of 2½, made the long journey from London through South East England and the Midlands to install Prince Edward in his new home. 'They travelled through slow stages,' Philippa Gregory imagines in *The White Queen*. 'Edward is strong but he is not yet three years old and riding all day is too tiring for him.' In *A Secret Alchemy*, Emma Darwin describes how the growing boy had 'the promise of his father's great height in his long-fingered little hands' that gripped the reins of the horse on the family's journey.

When Edward arrived at Ludlow in the spring of 1473 the castle was getting on for being four centuries old. Little substantial building work

CASTLE PLAN & KEY

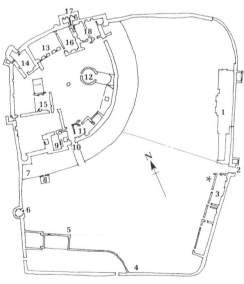

1 Castle House
2 Outer Gatehouse (Main Entrance)
3 Tudor Buildings (Shop & Gallery)
4 Curtain Wall
5 St Peter's Chapel
6 Mortimer's Tower
7 Castle Ditch
8 Ice House
9 Great Tower/Gatehouse Keep
10 Entrance to the Inner Bailey
11 Judges' Lodgings
12 Chapel of St Mary Magdalene
13 Great Hall
14 Solar Wing
15 Great Kitchen
16 Great Chamber Block
17 Garderobe Tower
18 Tudor Lodgings

*Information, Toilets, Gift Shop

Plan of Ludlow Castle. (*Source, Ludlow Castle*)

has been carried out since Edward's time, and much of what can be seen today by visitors would have been familiar to the prince. This includes the castle's basic ground plan, with its outer bailey wrapping almost wholly around the inner bailey; the great Norman Tower standing guard over the entrance to the inner bailey; the distinctive round chapel of St Mary Magdalene, situated within the inner bailey; and the Great Hall and its neighbouring administrative and residential ranges, their windows looking out over the inner bailey in one direction, and across the River Teme and towards the distant hills of Wales in the other. What has changed since the late Middle Ages is that all of this now lies in ruins, substantial to be sure, though most of the former rooms now lack roofs and floors, which were lost (along with large parts of the walls) in the centuries since the castle lost its political role in the 1680s.

As we have seen, the castle was initially constructed between 1085 and 1120 by Walter, Roger and Hugh de Lacy, as part of William the Conqueror's attempts to quell the Welsh borderlands. The de Lacys were responsible for the Keep and the walls surrounding what is now the inner bailey. Timber structures would have formed the living quarters within the original castle, though any evidence for these has long since vanished. But within the inner bailey was one stone building, the free-standing round Chapel of Mary Magdalene, and this survives to this day. The design of the building, with a rectangular chancel adjoining a circular nave, is seen in no other castle chapel in England, which makes the building Ludlow's most distinctive structure. The church was erected a little after the rest of the Norman castle, and was influenced in its design by the rotunda (*anastasis* in Greek) that was built over the rock-cut tomb of Jesus that formed part of the Church of the Holy Sepulchre in Jerusalem. This circular chapel was much admired by knights on the First Crusade, who first set eyes on it in 1099; some brought the architectural innovation back to Europe, among them Simon de Senlis, the First Earl of Northampton, who built England's first circular church – the Church of the Holy Sepulchre in Northampton – in around the year 1110. Ludlow's round chapel was built shortly after this, and was possibly initiated by Gilbert de Lacy, Roger's son, who went on pilgrimage to the Holy Land and later joined the Knights Templar. Although the chapel's present condition owes much to a comprehensive remodelling in the sixteenth century, when it gained a castellated roof, in its basic form it would have been familiar to Edward Plantagenet and would probably have been his principal place of

The Norman keep is the oldest part of Ludlow Castle.

prayer, as the castle's second (and later) chapel lay somewhat further away from the castle's main residential quarters.

The first great expansion of the castle came in the latter part of the same century, when the construction of an outer wall quadrupled the size of the castle and created the outer bailey, pierced by a new entrance that

The Chapel of Mary
Magdalene in Ludlow Castle
is the only circular castle
chapel in England.

The Chapel of Mary
Magdelene in Ludlow castle,
with the Tudor Lodgings –
which replaced the lodgings
where Edward Plantagenet
was brought up – to the left.

led onto Ludlow's market square – today's entrance for visitors. At this time too the original entrance tower (to this day the castle's most solid and substantial feature) was converted into a sturdy Keep, while a new entrance to the inner bailey from the outer bailey was cut through the curtain wall to its east, accessed by a new stone bridge across the former moat; today it is this elegant stone bridge and arched gate that are used by visitors to access the inner bailey from the outer, and this would have been the case too during the time of Edward Plantagenet.

Around seventy years after this construction work the castle came into the possession of Geoffrey de Geneville, a knight who married Maud de Lacy, a descendent of the family that originally built the castle. Geoffrey, Lord of Ludlow from 1251 to his death in 1283, set about rebuilding and extending the castle still further, adding a range of buildings overlooking the inner bailey that were constructed hard up against the castle's northern walls. These were the Great Hall and the 'Solar', the latter a name given to a suite of administrative and residential rooms that were built above a pantry and buttery that had direct access to the adjacent Hall. Today the Great Hall is one of the most evocative spaces in the castle. Reached by a heavily restored flight of steps that lead up from the inner bailey, the Hall lacks its floor – the undercroft below, like the hall itself, lies exposed to the sky – yet it is not difficult to imagine the noise and spectacle of the feasts that were held here. On its northern side the Hall abuts the castle's curtain wall, its windows looking over the river and, beyond, the Shropshire countryside. As we have already seen, Geoffrey's granddaughter married Roger Mortimer, the first Earl of March, and when Roger took possession of the castle in 1308 he set about completing the great range of buildings begun by Geoffrey, adding the Great Chamber Block to the east of the Great Hall. This block had large rooms, ornate fire places and luxurious sanitation facilities and was intended for the lord and lady of the castle and their immediate family, with accommodation for their guests on the floors above; with the Solar and the Great Hall, these three adjoining ranges, built in a near-continuous round of construction work that stretched from the 1270s to the 1320s, are today the most substantially surviving of all the castle's buildings, with the exception of the Keep.

These additions – particularly the Great Chamber Block – converted what had been an ordinary castle into a regal palace, as befitted the Mortimer family, who were now the most powerful landowners in England.

Ludlow Castle - the Solar, a residential and administrative wing built in the mid to late thirteenth century.

The Great Hall at Ludlow Castle is nowadays devoid of a roof and floor.

The building work also significantly altered the castle's profile when seen from the banks of the river; now, towers and chutes and battlements sprouted organically from the defensive knuckle of rock on which the castle stood, functional yet emblematic. This was a definite nod to Arthurian codes of yore (appropriately, as Roger Mortimer claimed descent from King Arthur through his great-grandfather, Prince Llywelyn Fawr, and was given to holding courtly gatherings at Ludlow around a symbolic Round Table). It was during Roger's time that Ludlow became a 'show' castle as much as a defensive one, after the fashion of the day – a fashion that was to reach its apogee in castles such as Bodiam, in Sussex, constructed in the 1380s by a subsequent generation of chivalric dreamers, where the defences were all show and the walls expressed power and prestige as much as they did an obstacle to be reckoned with by attackers.

Roger Mortimer was responsible for two more buildings in the castle, both abutting the outer curtain wall and so rather detached from the castle 'proper'. The first is St Peter's Chapel, the castle's second ecclesiastical building, built to commemorate his escape from the Tower of London in 1321 (he drugged his guards at a banquet). This chapel was later extended and converted into a courthouse – the Courthouse of the Council of the Marches – by Sir Henry Sidney in late Elizabethan times. Today its ruins can be best seen from the footpath that runs around the external perimeter of the castle, and which here briefly cuts inside the curtain walls. The other building from Mortimer's time is the tower that bears his name and is cut into the curtain wall of the castle, which is now, like the rest of the castle, unroofed, and in ruins.

Edward IV made a few improvements to the castle he had known so well as a boy; records show that in 1464–6 he paid £32 1s 8d for general repairs to the castle, and it is probable that he ordered the north face of the Norman keep and tower to be rebuilt during (or just before) his son took up residence. Edward probably always intended Ludlow to be the place where his first-born son would be brought up – and many of his improvements were to the interior décor, including the installation of richly decorated doorways, such as those giving access to the Keep and the one linking the Great Chamber and the Great Hall. It was probably through this grand doorway that Edward Plantagenet, then just 5 years old, made a ceremonial entrance in February 1476, during a great congress of the Marcher barons held at Ludlow. During his time at the castle Prince Edward would have prayed at St Peter's Chapel and at the great circular chapel of St Mary Magdalene, which still sits prominently in the courtyard of the inner bailey; he would have taken meals in the Great Hall and as he grew older he would have been involved in the administrative decisions taken in the adjacent Great Chamber Block. He would have conversed with the guards in Mortimer's Tower and the great Keep – perhaps even, as was the wont of medieval boys of his age and rank, it was from here that he flew his hawks. However, the private rooms where Edward was lodged have not survived; these, thought to have been situated between the Great Chamber Block and the Norman Pendover Tower, were demolished in the 1530s to make way for a new set of residential and administrative quarters associated with Ludlow's role as the Headquarters of the Council of Wales and the Marches. The block – marked today on castle plans as 'Tudor Lodgings' – once included a council chamber and a bridge that spanned part of the inner bailey, linking this range of buildings with a first-floor gallery in the round chapel. All that remains today of the original range

The Tudor Lodgings, which replaced the lodgings where Edward Plantagenet was brought up.

of buildings that Edward knew are the windows cut into the exterior walls on the northern side, that the prince would have once gazed out from over the beautiful Teme valley.

Making the Boy Who Will be King

Edward was still a toddler when he came to Ludlow: it was intended that his role in politics and decision making would develop as he became older. In July 1471, when he had been created Prince of Wales, a Council had been convened to make decisions concerning his welfare. Two years later, on 20 February 1473, just before Edward was moved to his new residence in Ludlow, this Council was enlarged and its remit enhanced, to give it an official political and judicial role over the Marches. Council members included Richard, Duke of Gloucester, who of course was to loom large in the story of Edward and his younger brother; Queen Elizabeth, the Princes' mother; the Archbishop of Canterbury and a number of other senior clergymen; William, Lord Hastings, chamberlain to Edward IV and one of his most loyal nobles, whose family had held important positions in government for generations; and a number of other lawyers and royal administrators.

At the Head of the council was John Alcock, a Yorkshire-born career clergyman who served as Bishop of Worcester, Rochester and Ely in succession, and who was twice appointed Lord Chancellor of England. Along with his official position as President of the Council, Alcock also served as tutor to Prince Edward (and later Prince Richard too). According to the king's ordinances concerning Edward, Alcock was required to 'teach and inform our said son in all spiritual cunning and virtue', though it appears that other tutors were employed for the boys' day-to-day tuition; one was John Giles, a professional schoolmaster, who from 20 May 1476 was given £20 per year for tutoring both Edward and Richard in French and Latin, though how this worked out given that the two boys were living over a hundred miles apart is unclear. In public life Alcock distinguished himself not only as a clergyman and administrator but also as a benefactor with a lifelong interest in education; he was a major endower of Hull Grammar School (which had been founded in 1330 and existed in one guise or another until 2015) and in 1496 he founded Jesus College, Cambridge, today one of the largest and most prestigious colleges of Cambridge University; the college still sports its emblem of a cockerel, chosen by Alcock as a reference to his own surname. In the narrative of the princes, Alcock distinguishes himself as the only one of Edward's close associates who did not meet his end at the hands of Richard of Gloucester in 1483; in fact Alcock was with Richard when the latter entered the city of York in triumph soon after his coronation. Many have used this as evidence of Richard's innocence in the princes' death, since, they argue, someone so close to the princes when they were alive would never have demonstrated such support for a man whom he knew to be their murderer.

With the Prince's Council assuming an increasingly wider role in law-making and regulation-setting in the Marches, a single figure was needed to oversee Edward's upbringing. Sir Thomas Vaughan was to look after the young boy's daily needs, as he had done at Westminster; he was put in charge of the prince's private apartments at Ludlow and oversaw the castle's upper household staff, who would attend on the prince every day. But Vaughan's role was a domestic one; he had no hand in guiding Prince Edward as he grew to be a boy and a young man, and a king-in-waiting. So it was decided that a 'master' be appointed, who would oversee Edward's welfare. This, in fact, was something of a tradition; since the time of the Norman Conquest the English royal family had appointed knights and (from the early 1400s) peers of the realm to act as 'masters' to oversee the development of the heir to the throne. In the case of Edward Plantagenet, the man chosen to 'guide the Prince in truth, honour, cunning, virtue and knightly demeanour', as King Edward's own ordinances had it, was the prince's maternal uncle Anthony Woodville, Earl Rivers, who was appointed the boy's governor on 10 November 1473, eight days after Edward's third birthday. The use of the terms 'governor' rather than 'master' was new – perhaps adopted because the latter term was coming to be associated with lowly schoolmasters, and the setting down of the governor's specific functions meant that this position could now be described as an 'office' within the royal household. Because Edward was Prince of Wales and Rivers would reside with him at Ludlow, the 'Prince's Governor' was not only a member of the Royal Council, but also had a unique and separate role involving the governing of the Welsh Marches on behalf of the king. Some have argued that this made Rivers the *de facto* ruler of Wales.

Rivers was 31 at the time of his appointment and had already distinguished himself in multiple fields. He was a soldier and a scholar, a man of renowned piety, chivalry and valour who was also prepared to use his shrewd political skills to advance himself; and what advancement he could expect, when young Edward reached the age of 18 and would naturally reward, in wealth and titles, the man who had overseen his own upbringing! Rivers is a fascinating figure and much has been written about him, both by his contemporaries and since. According to Dominic Mancini he was 'a kindly, serious and just man … and one tested by every vicissitude of life. Whatever his prosperity, he had injured nobody, though benefiting many.' Rivers was a veteran of a number of military campaigns, had distinguished himself at the age of 27 in a tournament with the preposterously titled Grand Bastard of Burgundy, and was rumoured to express his piety by wearing a hair shirt beneath his robes. For the first few years of his governorship Rivers' supervision of both Edward and the Marches was somewhat distant, as he was busy travelling in Europe, either on military campaign or devout pilgrimage to Santiago de Compostella, Portugal and Brittany; on a visit to Rome he was appointed Defender and Director of Papal Causes in England by Pope Sixtus IV. (There are even reports that he was planning to lead a crusade to the Holy Land.) Later on during his ten years overseeing the prince's upbringing at Ludlow, Rivers found time to translate three devotional works from Latin into French, which were printed together by William Caxton in 1477 as *The Dictes and Sayings of the Philosophers*. In the manuscript still held at Lambeth Palace there's a coloured miniature depicting a ceremony in which the earl presents the book to King Edward and his son, the latter (then aged 6) distinguished by his fair, wavy collar-length hair. Yet there was more to Rivers' appointment even than this; for one of the most vital positions he held was as the Queen's brother – and she was determined that he would bring Edward up to be a Woodville as much as a prince and a future king of England. Rivers would always champion the Woodville cause in the appointments he made to Edward's household – something that was to lead to catastrophic factional fighting when King Edward IV died, and the Woodvilles and their bitter opponents vied to control the boy-king Edward V and through him, England.

When the catastrophe struck, Rivers was the lynchpin of the Woodville faction. No wonder then, given his powerful position, he has excited the attention of novelists as well as historians. Emma Darwin makes him one of the principal protagonists of her novel *A Secret Alchemy*, in which Rivers, on the eve of his execution at Pontefract Castle, looks back on the role he has played in bringing up Edward, who by then is languishing in Richard of Gloucester's custody. 'Who could be more fit for such a great task than his uncle?' King Edward had told him early in the novel. 'You shall have the teaching of him in book-learning and at arms, and thanks to your knighthood my heir shall be the greatest prince in Christendom.' For his part, Rivers considered himself to be 'a young man [who] knew little of the governing of children. I did not know what it may do to even a young man's heart to have a little boy of some three summers sit on his saddlebow and sob for the leaving of his mother and sisters.' In Philippa Gregory's novel *The White Queen*, Rivers is portrayed in similarly noble terms, telling his sister the queen that he would,

> promise to bring up the boy as you and our family would wish … I can keep him to his learning and to his sports. I can teach him what he will need to be a good king of York. And it is something, to raise a king. It is a legacy to leave: that of making the boy who will be king.

Edward Plantagenet at Ludlow: The Schoolboy Prince

The specific way that the 'boy who will be king' should be 'made' was set down by King Edward IV in a set of royal ordinances issued on 27 September 1473, when Edward was nearly 3 years old (and re-issued ten years later on 25 February 1483, in a revised format that anticipated the boy's impending adolescence). The personal regimen prescribed by the 1473 ordinances was 'to be set up and begun at the Feast of Saint Michael the Archangel next following'. In these ordinances King Edward prescribed his son's daily routine almost minute-by-minute; no one was in any doubt as to when, where, and in what manner Edward should be studying, eating and praying while he was at Ludlow. (The original ordinances still exist, and are kept in the Public Record Office at Kew.) The ordinances provide both a set of rules that a strict but loving father expected to be followed, and a blueprint for the intense education of an aristocratic boy in the late Middle Ages. Although heirs to the throne had in the past been supplied with special households, nurses, chamberlains and tutors, Edward Plantagenet's upbringing differed in terms of how much it was deliberately and formally planned in advance through the ordinances, with a rigorous and precise division of each day. This stipulation that each day should be divided into clearly defined periods of activity came about in part because more precise ways of measuring time had been developed in the fifteenth century, marked by the proliferation of mechanical clocks in noble households and churches; along with this ability to tell the time precisely came a more sophisticated concept of how time should be divided and used, particularly in the field of education – it is thought that schools began operating to timetables in the 1440s, and universities shortly after.

In *The White Queen* Philippa Gregory has Queen Elizabeth musing that her eldest son loved living in Ludlow Castle, 'for he could ride into the hills and see the peregrine falcons soaring high above the cliffs, and he could swim in the cold water of the river … he had a good sense of landscape. Rare in the young.' (There are echoes here of Housman and his Arcadian view of a Shropshire childhood.) But how often did Edward have time for falconry and idle swimming? 'We purpose by God's grace,' the king wrote in his ordinances, 'to purvey that he shall be so virtuously, cunningly and knightly brought up to serve Almighty God, Christianly and devoutly, as accords to his duty, and to live and proceed in the world honourably after his estate and dignity.' The day was to start early – perhaps reflecting the fact that boys attending medieval schools were expected to be at their desks at six in the morning. 'We will that our said first-begotten son shall arise every morning at a convenient hour,' King Edward wrote. Glorious, of course, in mid-summer, but rather different in winter, when – in the words of Mark T.J. Griffin, whose novel *Richard of Eastwell* is partly set during Edward Plantagenet's upbringing in Ludlow – the air around the town would often be 'still with a biting icy chill, one which reaches the bones and gnaws at the marrow … [and] the hills around [Ludlow would be] dusted white [with snow]'. Presumably on days like these a fire would be burning in the Prince of Wales' rooms to take the chill off a bitter wind blowing from mountains of his principality.

'Till he be ready,' the ordinances continued,

> no man be suffered to come into chamber, except the right trusty the Earl Rivers, his chaplains, and chamberlains, or such others as shall be thought by the said Earl Rivers convenient for the same season; which chaplains shall say matins in his presence; and, when he is ready, and the matins

said, forthwith to go to his chapel or closet, to have his mass there, and not in his chamber without a reasonable cause; and no man is to interrupt him during a mass time.

Breakfast and school lessons then followed. 'We will that our said son have his breakfast immediately after his mass, and between that and his meat, shall be occupied in such virtuous learning as his age shall suffer to receive.' It is likely that Edward would have taken his lessons with a few other aristocratic boys who had been sent by their parents to Ludlow to be educated in Latin and Greek and to be schooled in knightly conduct; the only one whose name we know was Edmund Audley, the son of Lord Audley, who died in 1478 when Edward was 8 years old. Edmund Audley's family clearly considered his membership of the prince's household to have been an honour, for on the young man's tomb was declared that he had been the prince's sword-bearer and 'henchman' (or noble retainer).

Meals were always formal and ceremonial, with grace sung by Edward's own choristers. In the afternoon the boy needed to be 'at his dinner at a convenient hour, and thereat to be honourably served, and his dishes to be borne by worshipful folks and squires ... then [should] be read before him such noble stories as behoveth a prince to understand and know.' After this worthy bout of story-listening came lessons in knightly conduct: the boy should 'be showed all such convenient disports and exercises, as behoveth his estate to have experience in'. Evensong followed, presumably in the castle's round chapel, then dinner and bed.

> We will that our son go to his even-song at a convenient hour, and that soon after done, to be at his supper, and thereat to be served according as before. We will that our said son be in his chamber, and for all night livery [bread and ale] to be set, the travers [curtains] drawn anon upon eight of the clock [the 1483 ordinances moved this to 9 pm], and all persons from thence then to be avoided, except such as shall be deputed and appointed to give their attendance upon him all night; and that they enforce themselves to make him merry and joyous towards his bed.

Throughout this busy schedule (the arrangements varied according to the season, and separate arrangements applied when Edward was travelling), the boy was never left unattended; in fact the king's second ordinances of 1483 stipulated that Edward was to be accompanied everywhere by two 'discreet and convenient persons'. The prince would have been surrounded at various times by his chamberlain, his servants, his mentors, and by the carefully selected companions of his own age who shared his schooling, who would know their station and their role in making sure that 'the communication at all times in [Edward's] presence be of virtue, honour, cunning [knowledge], wisdom, and deeds of worship, and of nothing that should move or stir him to vice'; no 'swearer, brawler, backbiter, common hazarder or adulterer' were allowed into the household. Of the other boys in the household, the 'sons of nobles, lords and gentlemen', the ordinances decreed that they should also get up early and be 'taught in grammar, music and other cunning [knowledge] and exercise of humanity according to their births and ages, and in no wise to be suffered in idleness or in unadventurous occupation.' The boys and adults whom Edward associated with could be dismissed if they fell short of the standards the King expected. Edward had to mind his own behaviour too: the ordinances of 1483 stated that he was not to order anything to be done without the advice of Bishop Alcock, Earl Rivers or his councillor Sir Richard Grey, and none of his servants were to encourage him to conduct himself in a manner that was contrary to the ordinances, all of which suggests that Edward did assert himself at times – as any ordinary lively boy might. If he acted in an unprincely way he was warned personally of his behaviour, and if he refused to amend his ways the matter would be reported to his father, though what sanctions existed to correct any of a young boy's natural rambunctiousness is unclear. In Emma Darwin's *A Secret Alchemy* Rivers remembers how Edward 'got into mischief, as did the other children of the household, and was whipped for it,' which sounds plausible – though where Edward found the time and place to get himself into mischief is to be wondered at. A watch was even kept over him through the night in case sudden illness carried off the boy whom King Edward's ordinances claimed was 'God's precious sending and gift ... the King's most desired treasure.'

The regime seems to have paid off. Dominic Mancini observed, on one of Edward's visits to London, how well-read the boy was, with a good knowledge of books unless they were from 'among the more abstruse authors'. (Edward's fondness for books was celebrated by William Caxton, who dedicated his *History of Jason* to the Prince, so that he may 'begin to learn to read English' from it, and assimilate the tales of noble deeds as he did so.) Mancini also observed how Edward 'devoted himself to horses and dogs and other useful exercises to invigorate his body' – these would have included archery and tourney, the latter involving exercises in swordsmanship, wearing armour.

Novelists have played on Edward's reputation for both scholarliness and manliness (the very image, of course, of his uncle Anthony). In *A Secret Alchemy* Emma Darwin recounts how when Elizabeth visited Ludlow she found Edward healthy from his,

> knightly exercises in these long, warm days. He was proud to show me his skill at the quintain [training for jousting, using a lance] and when I asked how his studies went, even prouder of his translation of Horace. At my bidding he read a few sentences, and if he stumbled once or twice, it was only from shyness, not ignorance.

Philippa Gregory, also telling her story from Queen Elizabeth's point of view, remarks that Edward comes across as 'a serious little boy, thoughtful, and he offers to read to me in Latin, Greek or French until I confess that his learning far surpasses my own.' If the book-learning came from Bishop Alcock and other tutors, the soldiery came from Rivers, an experienced knight and jouster, who might have taught the boy these skills himself. In *A Secret Alchemy* Emma Darwin shows how Rivers,

> sure that [Edward] understood what his father knew of how a Kingdom is secure ... not his father's way with others' wives, for he was mercifully late in getting an eye for a wench ... he has learnt to fence and dance and hunt ... though even Ned had to be tempted to his desk, when the sun was out over the Teme and he had a new horse to try.'

Piety was also something Edward gained a reputation for – presumably under the influence of Earl Rivers and Bishop Alcock. As he faces his imminent execution, Darwin has Earl Rivers remembering how he 'sometimes watched [Edward] kneeling before the Host at Mass and my heart sang to see my boy lost so well in the love of God.'

Edward's personal education was just one part of the ordinances issued by Edward IV. The second part directed the conduct of Edward's household, and included such stipulations as the gates of the castle being locked from 9 pm to 6 am between the feast of Michaelmas (29 September) and 1 May, and from 10 pm to 5 am in the lighter months; another regulation set down that if any person in the household should 'strike another within the house' or 'draw any weapon ... in violence', he was to be sent to the stocks for the length of time decided by the council for a first offence, and lose office for a second. Edward's household at Ludlow numbered around fifty and included esquires, ushers and clerical staff, in addition to an almoner, two chaplains and a group of boy choristers who sung in the prince's chapel (as well as at the start of meals). All this was to be paid for by moneys collected from the Duchy of Cornwall, the Principality of Wales and the Earldom of Chester and Flint, all of which estates Edward had held more or less since birth. According to the ordinances only three people held the keys to the prince's coffers in which all the money was kept – namely 'our dearest wife the Queen', Bishop Alcock and Earl Rivers.

King of England

At Ludlow Edward Plantagenet was raised to be king. But no one around him could have guessed that he would assume the mantle of kingship so young. His father had, for the most part, been healthy and fit, and it seemed unlikely that he would die before his time, leaving the throne to a minor and, although it was true that the king in middle-age had become corpulent and slow, his death on 9 April 1483 was still wholly unexpected.

So when 'the king's messengers arrived at Ludlow, mud-spattered and weary' some five days later, the news they brought came as a bolt from the blue. In *A Secret Alchemy*, Emma Darwin goes on to recount how news of the king's death was conveyed by the mud-spattered messengers to Earl Rivers in the castle courtyard. Not surprisingly he hesitates on hearing it; but he sees 12-year-old Edward across the courtyard, and knows the task that awaits him.

> When I spoke, my boy would know himself to be Edward, by the grace of God King of England and France and Lord of Ireland ... try as I must – for the business of the kingdom

waited on it – I could not bring myself to step forward and tell
him what he had become ... I stood for one more moment,
watching my boy in the last, laughing air of his boyhood.

Edward approaches him and blathers boyishly something about mummers
having arrived in Ludlow, and could they go and watch them. Rivers
ignores his breathless plea, and steps forward. 'Sire, your father the king
is dead. By God's grace, long may you live and reign.' The boy stands
spellbound as Rivers kneels before him.

The messengers from London carried with them not only the news
of King Edward's death, but also a letter from the Royal Council asking
Rivers to bring the new king to London by 1 May for his coronation.
Edward was now sovereign. But as a minor, ascending the throne at a
time of political turmoil, he was just a cypher; the Woodvilles saw him
as their instrument, their means to dominate England politically, and
their foes were already bitterly resenting this. Anxious to prevent matters
from overheating, Elizabeth agreed that Edward's escort as he travelled to
London be limited to 2,000 men. Soldiers began gathering immediately;
Marcher men from the local area, loyal to the new king who had been
brought up in their midst. Dominic Mancini recounts that on 16 April,
two days into his kingship, Edward himself wrote to the burghers of Lynn
in Norfolk that he intended to be 'at our city of London in all convenient
haste, by God's grace to be crowned at Westminster', and quite possibly as
he wrote these words, the clatter of wheelwrights and carpenters and the
clang of armourers and blacksmiths could be heard from Ludlow Castle's
outer bailey as preparations were made for the journey.

A week later, on 23 April, the castle hosted celebrations for St George's
Day when, according to the Tudor chronicler John Rous, 'the accustomed
service of the Knights of the Garter was solemnly celebrated, concluding
with a splendid banquet'. Edward, king though not yet crowned, must
have taken centre stage in these celebrations, which would have begun
with a solemn service in the castle's round Chapel of St Mary Magdalene,
after which the celebrants would have walked a short distance across the
castle's inner bailey and up the steps to the Great Hall, where they sat
down to the spectacular feast that awaited them. By then the preparations
for the journey were complete; the following morning a great procession,
which presumably gathered in the castle's spacious outer bailey, headed
out of the castle and through Ludlow's market square, with Edward at

its head and Bishop Alcock, Sir Thomas Vaughan and Earl Rivers close behind him. The first stage of their journey to London had begun.

St Laurence's Church

Visitors expecting to catch a first glimpse of Ludlow castle when they emerge from the train at the town's small railway station will find themselves disappointed. The castle is not visible from the eastern part of the town, where the station is situated. Instead, it is the tall, elegant, russet-red square tower of St Laurence's Church that draws the eye of those newly arrived by train, a beacon on a nearby hill that marks the position of Ludlow's old town. Situated just off the market square, and barely a minute's walk from the castle entrance, the tower of the church is today visible from miles around, just as it was in the late Middle Ages. The redness comes from the local sandstone used to build it; some 300 million years ago the land now covered by Shropshire's lush countryside was an arid desert, and the tower was fashioned from what remains of that desert, in the form of new red sandstone blocks that were quarried from Felton, a couple of miles upstream from Ludlow along the River Corve. But the conspicuousness of the tower comes from its height and its handsome proportions, not its hue. Its prominence in the landscape is celebrated most famously in *The Recruit*, part of A.E. Housman's *A Shropshire Lad*, in which a young soldier is sent on his way to war with the exhortation 'Go and luck go with you / While Ludlow Tower shall stand.' Housman was born in Worcestershire, and had not even visited his Shropshire Eden when he wrote his epic verse cycle, yet the burial of his ashes in the shadow of the tower of St Laurence's Church, and the erection of a memorial plaque to him on the exterior wall of the church (beside a cherry tree, celebrated in another poem in *A Shropshire Lad*), seems to sanctify an almost transcendental homecoming.

Just like the castle, the origins of St Laurence's Church go back to Norman times. Before then the location was possibly used as a burial site; records suggest that structures such as tumuli stood here, though no evidence of them remains. Little evidence remains too of the earliest incarnations of the church; the original Norman construction and the extensive rebuilding work carried out in 1199 were both obliterated by the subsequent series of large-scale rebuilding projects initiated by Ludlow's wealthy elite of tradesmen and merchants, which resulted in the creation of one of the largest and most beautiful parish churches in the country. Indeed St Laurence's is one of only eighteen churches to be awarded a five-star rating by Simon Jenkins in his popular book *England's Thousand Best Churches,* and the church's Palmers' Guild window even features on the cover of the book's first edition. The church plays an important part in the history of Ludlow and has a walk-on role to play in the story of Edward Plantagenet and his kin, too.

Late medieval Ludlow was well endowed with religious foundations. In addition to the two chapels in the castle, the Augustinian and Carmelite orders maintained their own friaries, and beside Ludford Bridge was the Hospital of St John of Jerusalem, a religious house that, in the manner of all medieval 'hospitals', provided shelter for travellers and sustenance for the poor as well as care (and even basic medical treatment) for the sick. In 1478 Richard, Duke of Gloucester, promoted one of his former chaplains to the position of Prior here; Richard required the Prior (or another of the hospital's brethren) to celebrate mass on a regular basis for Prince Edward in St Peter's Chapel in the castle, and the appointment reflects the close ties that Richard had with Ludlow, which he visited on a number of occasions while his nephew was residing here. But the focus of the town's religious life was St Laurence's – and it was the focus of the town's patrician life too, as most prominent citizens belonged to the Palmers' Guild, whose foundation and activities were inextricably bound up with the church. The Guild, founded as the Guild of St Mary and St John in the thirteenth century, though popularly named after the palm fronds that pilgrims traditionally brought back from the Holy Land, was expensive to join and conferred status upon its members. Benefits they enjoyed included a rudimentary form of insurance (against the roof of their home caving in, for instance). But the Guild saw its primary purpose as supporting St Laurence's, particularly in its funding of the priests who served there, along with four singing men, two deacons, six choristers, and a porter. By the fifteenth century the Guild was a powerful and influential body whose members included prominent local figures such as Sir Edmund Mortimer, the last Mortimer Earl of March, who attended their annual feast in 1424, and his successor Richard Plantagenet, Duke of York, who became a Guild member along with his wife in 1437; by that time Guild members were spread as far as the West Midlands and Bristol.

Although the Guild was dissolved in 1551 its name lives on today in the form of a charity run by the church.

It was the Palmers' Guild that was instrumental in the reconstruction work carried out at St Laurence's between 1434 and 1471, which saw the church rebuilt in the soaring perpendicular style fashionable at the time. The extensive work (and the resulting size of the church, which is often referred to as the 'Cathedral of the Marches') reflects both the wealth and influence of the town's commercial elite and Ludlow's growing political importance under Richard Plantagenet, Duke of York, and then his son Edward IV, whose regranting of Ludlow's charter in 1461 gave a considerable fillip to the town's sense of self-confidence. John Leland considered the newly rebuilt church to be 'very fair and large and richly adorned, and taken for the fairest in all these parts', when he visited it in 1540. The most distinctive feature added during the fifteenth-century rebuild was the tower, though all we know of its builder was that he was a mason from Gloucester. Some of the interior decoration installed in the fifteenth century remains to this day, most notably the choir stalls with their finely carved misericords – decorative carvings on the underside of folding wooden seats – that can be firmly dated to 1447. The carvings depict the social and commercial activities of Ludlow – one, for instance, shows a character known as Simon the Cellarer decanting beer from a bowl into a jug – though there are heralds too, and one misericord depicts Richard Plantagenet's personal emblem of a fetterlock (a shackle resembling a modern-day padlock) and a falcon (the latter being the emblem of the Plantagenets). The celebrated Palmers' Guild window was also added at this time, as was another fine stained-glass window showing the life, miracles and martyrdom of St Laurence.

Edward Plantagenet must have prayed at St Laurence's from time-to-time, making the short journey from the castle to the church in the company of his uncle. It is also possible that the choristers who sung grace for Edward at the castle were drawn from the church (providing considerable kudos to the Palmers' Guild). Yet locating firm features in the church that form a visible link with Edward Plantagenet's residence in Ludlow are slim and rather tangential. His councillor John Sulyard, a member of the small committee that ran the day-to-day affairs of the Marches, and his servant Piers Beaupie, are both buried in the church; their grave markers have been lost (though they may be under the wooden plinths that support the pews – John Leland recorded seeing Beaupie's grave in 1540). Little is known about Sulyard but Beaupie was a prominent lawyer who also served as the town corporation's recorder and as MP for Ludlow; when he died in 1480 his widow founded a private chantry at the altar of St Gabriel and St Mary, situated close to the church's east wall, though like the other chantries established by the Palmers' Guild it has long since disappeared.

The most prominent link with Edward Plantagenet's time can be seen in the stained glass in the west window, designed by Thomas Willement Glass (1786–1871) and installed as part of the comprehensive Victorian redesign of the church interior. The window's lower part depicts four figures, each set within their own separate frame, and each representing a royal generation associated with Ludlow in the late fifteenth century: Richard Plantagenet, third Duke of York; his son King Edward IV; Edward Plantagenet himself, King Edward's son; and finally Prince Arthur, who was Edward IV's grandson (the son of his daughter Elizabeth) and a figure we shall see more of later. Suffice to say for now that Prince Arthur's 'heart' (a euphemism for his entrails) was buried in the church when he

Two heirs to the throne in the stained glass windows at St Laurence's Church, Ludlow – Edward Plantagenet and Arthur Tudor.

Edward Plantagenet as depicted in the Victorian stained glass windows at St Laurence's Church, Ludlow.

King Edward IV, as depicted in stained glass in St Laurence's Church. Edward was brought up in Ludlow Castle and sent his oldest son, Edward Plantagenet, to be brought up in the castle too.

died at Ludlow Castle in 1502, the position of the casket marked by a plaque (though attempts to find the lead box in which his bodily parts were laid to rest proved fruitless when searched for in the eighteenth century); the rest of him is in Worcester Cathedral. In the window Arthur is depicted at prayer; he wears a prominent crown and carries a sword on his hilt, his gown decorated in the fleur-de-lis and lions passant emblems that had been adopted as the Royal Arms of England by Edward III in the 1340s. Edward Plantagenet, in contrast, seems far less worldly, an ascetic figure of indeterminate age clad in a plain pale blue gown and a smock of pastel yellow. Both boys were Prince of Wales and both were first in line to the English throne. While neither was eventually crowned, Edward at least became king, if only for a short while; Arthur died well before he could assume the role history had marked out for him. Odd, then, that these nineteenth-century windows at Ludlow portray Arthur as by far the more regal of the two.

North, to Shrewsbury

Ludlow may have been a major commercial and political centre of the Welsh borderlands in the Middle Ages – but it was not the largest or most important of the string of fortress towns that protected England from the threat from the west. That honour belonged to Shrewsbury, 23 miles north of Ludlow, which had been a royal borough and military stronghold since the early rule of William the Conqueror (and before that had been the capital of the ancient Welsh Kingdom of Powys). Just after the Conquest, the Normans built a timber fort at Shrewsbury that was besieged in 1069 by an alliance of men from Wales and Chester. The men were fought off but it was clear to William that more robust defences were required. So he placed Shrewsbury under the command of his trusted ally Roger de Montgomery, who tore down the old timber castle and in its place constructed a sturdy stone castle that overlooked the town. Later, in 1083, with the castle complete, Roger founded the town's great abbey, and entered it some eleven years later as a monk, dying after just three days as a novice. Some 400 years later, at the time of King Edward IV, the abbey and the castle were still the two most important institutions in the town. But in the intervening centuries Shrewsbury had also gained at least four more churches, three friaries and two religious hospitals, and had also grown to become a major player in the wool trade, which was the backbone and driving force of the economy of late medieval England.

Shrewsbury has one of the most notable and distinctive ground plans of any English town. Its ancient core is situated on a hilly ridge that is almost entirely encircled by a great loop of the River Severn, crossed on each side by bridges. At the highest point of the ridge, guarding the vulnerable 'neck' in the river's loop, is the castle, rebuilt extensively over the centuries and now housing the Shropshire Regimental Museum (most noteworthy exhibit: a lock of Napoleon's hair). Enclosed within the defensive ring of river and castle is, according to Nikolaus Pevsner, 'England's finest Tudor town', its opulent buildings reflecting Shrewsbury's wool trading days. The town's dominance in this economic arena received royal approval in 1462 when Edward IV, always showing a keen interest in the Marches, incorporated by Royal Charter the Shrewsbury Drapers Company, which was to hold a virtual monopoly on the trade in Welsh cloth for the following three hundred years. Trade depended on favourable transport links; the Severn was navigable to Shrewsbury, and wool could be shipped easily downriver to Worcester, Gloucester and Bristol (this was the town's principal advantage over Ludlow in the wool trade, as the Teme, unlike the Severn, is not navigable by barges); meanwhile Watling Street, whose old Roman terminus was 5 miles downstream from Shrewsbury at Wroxeter (Roman Viroconium), offered the traders a route by road to London and continental Europe. With Shrewsbury's wealth came an urban swagger that Ludlow never had. Today, though, there's no trade on the River Severn, and the only vessels disturbing the waters of the river are tourist cruise boats and the rowing crews of Shrewsbury School (founded in 1552, at the height of the Tudor economic boom); and Shrewsbury's economy is based not on wool but on tourism, distribution, retailing and business parks – though the town has retained its brewing tradition, which dates back to the Middle Ages. Only recently has its military role, which lasted nearly 1,000 years, been abandoned; the one remaining barracks in the town sounded its last bugle call in 2014.

Shrewsbury's role in the story of the Princes in the Tower is significant, yet so much is gone from that era, so much of the detail is conjecture or supposition, that it is difficult to get a real idea of how anything that can be seen in the modern town contributes to a deeper understanding of their story. A good place to start, though, is the Market Hall at the heart of the town centre, built by the town's Corporation in 1596 to showcase Shrewsbury's economic good fortune. On the façade of the columned hall is the statue of an armoured man. Some say the man is Richard, third Duke of York, the military commander who was the father of Edward IV and the grandfather of the princes; if it is, then this is the only representation of Richard in existence (others maintain that the man with the sword is the Black Prince, son of Edward III). The statue originally stood on the gatehouse guarding the Old Welsh Bridge across the Severn; it was moved to the Market Hall in 1771, some two decades before that bridge was demolished to make way for the current one. Whether it is Richard of York or the Black Prince, the ascetic, somewhat forbidding statue reminds us that during the Middle Ages the Welsh Marches were a sensitive and often troubled border region, busy with garrisons and castles – which is partly why the region was chosen as the place where a future king of England should be sent to be raised.

This statue of an armoured man on the facade of the Market Hall in the centre of Shrewsbury might depict Richard Plantagenet, Third Duke of York, the grandfather of the princes.

Really, the castle should provide a firmer link to the late fifteenth century, but here, too, things are vague or smudged. By the time of Edward IV the castle was a neglected hulk, in a semi-ruined state with parts of its roof missing. During the ten years he lived at Ludlow Edward Plantagenet made a number of visits to Shrewsbury, and although it is entirely possible he resided at the castle, it seems more likely that Roger de Montgomery's great Benedictine abbey across the river would have been a more likely place to host the Prince of Wales and his entourage. Not only did the abbey have a roof, it was also famous for its lavish hospitality, championed by the long-serving abbot of the day, Thomas Mynde (1460–97). Today the abbey church is still there, but it's not a particularly graceful building (despite the original Norman arches in the nave) and it's wedged uncomfortably against the main approach road to the English Bridge, Shrewsbury's other great crossing over the Severn. The church is built from the local sandstone, and its most noteworthy treasure is a carved stone panel hanging in the nave that is reputedly all that remains of a shrine, brought here by monks in 1137, that commemorated St Winifred, the venerated daughter of an obscure seventh-century Welsh prince. As to the monastery buildings that once lay in the abbey's shadow – the monks' residential and administrative quarters – after Abbot Mynde's time the rot apparently set in, and the buildings were in a severe state of decay forty years after his death, when Thomas Cromwell's men turned up to dissolve the monastery and sell off its goods and chattels. In 1836 those monastic buildings that remained were demolished to make way for Thomas Telford's great new Holyhead road, now the abbey church's too-close-for-comfort traffic-clogged nemesis. All that remains of the buildings are the surreal remains of a pulpit, enclosed by a small garden, across the road from the abbey church and surrounded by a supermarket carpark. This grand pulpit was built in the fourteenth century by Abbot Nicholas Stevens as an addition to the abbey's refectory; the tiny garden surrounding it is inaccessible and the best view of this surreal structure is actually from the trains rumbling into Shrewsbury station from the south on a low-level viaduct that takes the railway across the main road.

The supermarket car park in which the unfortunate pulpit is marooned, and which covers the site of the former monastic buildings, dates from 1980, and before it was laid out archeologists were given a chance to see what they could salvage from the site. What was uncovered in the dig were the remains of an early fifteenth-century kitchen and a large rubbish dump

Shrewsbury Abbey; Edward Plantagenet probably stayed in the adjacent monastery when his younger brother was born in the town.

next to it that yielded a beguiling historical cocktail of human waste, stable sweepings and kitchen scrapings – though enough to allow archeologists to conclude that the monks feasted regularly on platters of game and fish. But amid all this, one real treasure was uncovered from these murky finds. It takes the form of a small bowl – nothing ornate, and resembling perhaps a soup bowl – that is the earliest example of hallmarked secular silver in the world. Dated to 1337, the bowl, now blackened with age, takes pride of place in the Shrewsbury Museum and Art Gallery, though curators relate with delight how the object has long been coveted by the British Museum. Other finds from the dig, also displayed in the museum, include a number of leather shoe soles, their survival guaranteed by being submerged in the waterlogged mud of the Severn.

Edward Plantagenet came to Shrewsbury – to worship in the abbey, pray at the shrine of St Winifred, and perhaps to eat from one of the abbey refectory's fine silver bowls while listening to a sermon delivered from its even finer pulpit – on a number of occasions. Town records show that in 1478 and 1480 the boy was given a gift of wine 'in honour of the town', while on 10 April 1481 Bishop Alcock, the President of the Council, accompanied by Earl Rivers and the 10-year-old prince, were at Shrewsbury Town Hall where they imposed a set of ordinances for the 'weal, rest and tranquility of the same town and for good rule to be kept by the officers, mysteries [guilds] and inhabitants thereof.' But the most momentous of Edward's stays came earlier than this, when, not yet 3 years old, he was present in Shrewsbury with his father while his mother gave birth to his baby brother.

The boy was christened Richard, in honour of his grandfather and uncle. He was born on 17 August 1473 in Shrewsbury's Dominican or Black Friary, a couple of minutes' walk from the abbey church, across the English Bridge. His mother was in the town as part of a wider tour of the Marches, supporting young Edward as he became established at Ludlow. (It has been suggested that Richard was born prematurely, before the queen had a chance to return to Ludlow or London, which would have been more suitable places to give birth.) Shrewsbury's community of Dominican monks, who were known as the Black Friars because of the black mantles they wore over their white habits, had arrived in the town in around 1230, shortly after the foundation of their order, and had established their religious house beside the river, close to the castle. In 1403 high-ranking victims of the Battle of Shrewsbury were buried in the abbey's churchyard, and in the same year that Richard Plantagenet was born there, Elizabeth Countess Rivers, the first wife of Earl Rivers, was also laid to rest following her untimely death. But the monastery was dissolved by Cromwell's henchmen in 1538 and (unlike the Benedictine Abbey) was immediately torn down; today no traces of it remain and the

The grassy bank in the middle distance was the site of Shrewsbury's Dominican Friary, where Richard Plantagenet, the younger of the princes, was born.

location is marked by nothing more exceptional than a grassy bank that rises from a pleasant riverside walk (busy with cyclists and joggers) to some smart flats (named the Blackfriars apartments, after the building that once stood here). There is nothing else. (A plaque might be nice: 'Richard Plantagenet, the younger of the Princes in the Tower, was born in the Dominican Friary that stood here, 17 August 1473'). Of all the places associated with the princes and their story, this is the one whose historical traces have been most decisively obliterated by the inexorable passage of time.

The Princes in Stained Glass: Little Malvern Priory and Canterbury Cathedral

Some 25 miles southeast of Ludlow, not far from the cathedral city of Worcester, is a dramatic spine of hills whose summits afford one of the best – and most classic – views of England. The highest of the bald, knuckle-like peaks is Worcestershire Beacon, rising to a lofty 425m and overlooking the venerable spa town of Great Malvern. From here, on a clear day, a 365-degree perspective takes in the spires of the three great cathedrals of Worcester, Hereford and Gloucester, shimmering in the distance amid the greenness of England. The glorious panorama takes in the plains of the West Midlands to the east – the agricultural West Midlands of *The Archers*, not the industrial West Midlands that lies beyond the horizon – while in the other direction folds of countryside seem to lap against the hills' western flanks, a sea of green that stretches to the Brecon Beacons, a grey-purple haze in the far distance beyond which lie the dour Welsh valley towns of Ebbw Vale and Merthyr Tydfil. This most English of scenes provided the inspiration for that most English of composers, Edward Elgar, and inspired a very English writer too, namely William Langland, whose 1362 poem *Piers Plowman* was partly set in this breathtaking landscape.

Elgar is buried in St Wulstan's church, tight up against the eastern flank of the Malvern Hills. Some 500yds away, and also tucked into the lowest fold of the hills, is one of England's most remarkable churches.

The Malvern Hills, close to Little Malvern Priory.

Little Malvern Priory began life as a monastery church in around 1127, during the reign of Henry I, whose royal hunting grounds spread across the plains to the east, towards the distant River Severn. In those days this was a wild and remote area. According to folklore the first monks who came here were Jocelin and Eldred, brethren from the great Benedictine monastery at Worcester. They were ascetics, intending to live in the shadow of the high hills as hermits. Even before their arrival this place may well have been a place of Christian worship, in Saxon and even Celtic times. Only the barest fragments of the original Norman church known to Jocelin and Eldred remain; much of what is seen of the building today dates from substantial rebuilding in the thirteenth century, when King Henry III donated ten oaks for its reconstruction, and from further building work carried out in the later Middle Ages. William Langland might well have been a pupil at the monastery's school at this time – though this is largely conjecture; many sources link him to the nearby monastery at Great Malvern rather than to the one here.

When the monastic foundation at Little Malvern was dissolved, the church and the surrounding land were sold to a powerful local family, the Russells. Their descendants still live in Little Malvern Court, the ivy-clad property that adjoins the church and which is just visible over the churchyard wall (the formal gardens are occasionally open to the public). Gradual ruination and abandonment of the church followed; in 1799 the antiquarian George Lipscomb, in his *Journey into South Wales,* was able to describe 'an old church crumbling into decay', and half a century later John Noake wrote of 'the deplorable condition of this once beautiful church' and complained of the 'injudicious repairs, mutilation and neglect' in his 1851 book *A Rambler in Worcestershire.* The roof collapsed in 1864. It was repaired, and piecemeal restoration work has continued since then; but today all that remains intact of the medieval priory church are the tower and chancel, the ruins of the adjacent transept being wide open to the sky. But the church is loved and cared for; in the shadow of the ruined walls is a neat, shady cemetery, with recent gravestones standing grey and sombre amid freshly cut grass, while a sign at the entrance notifies worshippers of the times of services (how many, one wonders, attend the 8 am Holy Communion on the second Sunday in the month – for there is no village here, just some farm buildings and smart villas beside the main road). In the 1960s a porch (with small pantry) was added to the church to form the present entrance; in one corner of this porch stands a simple statue, surrounded by fresh flowers, of a pious-looking cleric. The cleric is Bishop Alcock and it is he who provides this church's link with the Princes in the Tower.

Head through the door from the porch and you enter a gem of a church, with walls of bare stone; a small, simple place of rugged but restrained grandeur, kept spick and span, as these places are, by a small army of quietly proud and industrious local volunteers (one suspects that the fresh flowers around Bishop Alcock's statue are attended to by strict rota). This wasn't the state in which Bishop Alcock found the place on his visit in 1480 (was he accompanied here on this occasion by his tutorial charge, the 10-year-old Edward Plantagenet?). At the time, Alcock was the Bishop of Worcester and Little Malvern was part of his diocese; he was not happy with what he saw. The church was, he declared sadly, in a state of 'great ruin'; Alcock accused the monks and Prior of neglecting their curatorial duties and promptly sent them to Gloucester Abbey for a period of re-education. While the monks were away in Gloucester, Alcock set about

Statue of Bishop Alcock, tutor to the princes, in Little Malvern Priory.

rebuilding the church; when the holy brethren returned two years later they must have scarcely recognised the place. Alcock was an accomplished architect; when he founded Jesus College, Cambridge, his lasting legacy, he also supervised the substantial alterations that were made to the original priory that his new college buildings occupied – and his work at Little Malvern was similarly thorough. One of the architectural flourishes he created were the graceful linen-fold arches at the top of the pillars of the nave, which can still be admired today; but his major triumph was the glorious suite of glass in the East Window, in which Edward Plantagenet is depicted in vibrant colours.

The glass for this window was fashioned at the workshop of Richard Twygge and Thomas Woodshawe, well-regarded local craftsmen whose work also appears in Westminster Abbey and in the Magnificat window of Great Malvern Priory, just up the road from Little Malvern. Today only parts of their creation remain visible; the window was smashed either during the Dissolution or the Civil War, and when it was reconstructed, only some parts were salvageable. Of the six smaller lights that make up

The East Window in Little Malvern Priory, which shows Edward Plantagenet and his immediate family.

Edward Plantagenet depicted in the stained glass window at Little Malvern Priory.

Edward Plantagenet depicted in stained glass in St Matthew's Church, Coldridge, Devon.

the lower window, three are simply of clear glass, but the others show, from left to right, three kneeling figures – and the one on the left is Prince Edward. He is depicted as a kneeling, blonde-haired figure, his hands clasped in prayer and his lips nearly curled into a pious smile; he wears a red and white robe and a blue gown beneath, and he is oddly ageless. His younger brother would have occupied the light on the far left, while to the right would have been King Edward, facing his queen – whose hands and gown are visible today, but nothing else – and their daughters, whose window is as gloriously complete as the one that depicts Edward. The window on the far right, now clear, would have depicted Bishop Alcock himself, praying for the family. (We can surmise this as this was the standard arrangement for royal figures in windows such as this.) Alcock's dedication of the window survives at a lower level: 'Pray for the soul of John Alcock, Bishop of Worcester, who rebuilt this church … formerly Chancellor of England, and president of the Council of Edward IV.' His coat of arms, a mitre and cockerel heads, can be seen at the top right of the window, which would have also depicted saints and various armorial shields; the Royal Arms with its lions passant and fleur-de-lis (as at Ludlow) appears top left.

This depiction of Edward Plantagenet, made around 1481 when he was 12 years old, is one of only two contemporary representations of the prince in stained glass; as such it provides a tangible link with his life and times. To see the only other representation of Edward in stained glass that was also fashioned in his lifetime it's necessary to travel 100 miles south from Little Malvern, to the mid-Devon village of Coldridge. This village was once the property of Thomas Grey, the Marquess of Dorset, who was the eldest son of Elizabeth Woodville from her first marriage to the Leicestershire knight Sir John Grey, and who was therefore the half-brother to Princes Edward and Richard. In the 1470s the marquess was tasked by King Edward with bolstering royal authority in the West Country, hence his connections with this village; it is thought that Grey's park-keeper, Sir John Evans, may have installed the stained-glass memorial to Edward that can be seen today in Coldridge's St Matthew's Church. (Some sources maintain that the window here actually portrays Edward VI, rather than Edward V; but the book and sceptre the figure is shown with are more associated with fifteenth-century kings, and Edward VI issued a number of injections against stained glass windows, making it unlikely he would be portrayed in one.)

As to the other representations of Edward in stained glass, all are from later centuries. As we have seen, the 'Royal Window' in St Laurence's Church in Ludlow is wholly Victorian – though the window of the same name in Canterbury Cathedral makes more of a claim to being contemporary with Edward Plantagenet's time. It commemorates Edward's visit to Canterbury in 1481 in the company of his father, when king and 11-year-old prince prayed together at the Shrine of Thomas Becket and also reviewed the English fleet at nearby Sandwich. The window, fashioned by the esteemed craftsman William Neve, was probably built in 1483, just before Edward IV's death and his son's accession. In the window the king is depicted kneeling at a prayer desk emblazoned with an emblem of Saint George and the Dragon. He holds a sceptre and behind him is an emblem of the white rose of York *en soleil* – 'surrounded by the sun'. His eldest son Prince Edward, straight-backed and formal-looking, holds a mass book and wears a prominent crown and a robe of ermine. His own badge of the Prince of Wales' ostrich feathers, and motto *Ich Dien*, distinguish him from his younger brother Richard, who like his father and brother is depicted kneeling at a prayer desk; he is crowned and robed in purple with an ermine collar, and with the Plantagenet badge of a falcon and fetterlock to his left. However the heads of both princes are not original. In December 1642 the original window was badly damaged by Richard Culmer, a minister serving in the cathedral whose puritan zealotry led him to this act of vandalism. The heads of both boys are eighteenth-century replacements, which makes this window inferior to the one at Little Malvern in terms of its depiction of the princes. The window is built above the site of Becket's martyrdom, now marked by a stark contemporary memorial; in medieval times – before its destruction during the Reformation – Becket's actual shrine, where generations of kings and princes once prayed, including King Edward and his young son, was situated some distance away in the cathedral's choir.

Edward Plantagenet's Journeys from Ludlow: Coventry, Eltham and the Marches

Edward Plantagenet was a well-travelled prince. Though based at Ludlow from the age of 3 – his warrants were issued from there from 1474 onwards – his frequent trips away took him to various places in and around the Marches, the Midlands and South East England. Some of these trips took in the various estates and castles that had been gifted to him by his father; however, since these embraced holdings as far away as the remote west coast of Wales (the 'Principality') and Castle Rising in deepest Norfolk, it is highly unlikely the prince's travels would ever have taken him anywhere near these places. In contrast he made frequent visits to major centres in the Midlands and the Marches that were nearer to Ludlow, including Chester, the great cathedral city of the northern Welsh borderlands, and Hereford, its counterpart in the southern borderlands. One visit to Hereford came shortly after the birth of Edward's younger brother Richard, when records show that the two young princes, accompanied by their parents, travelled there from Shrewsbury via Ludlow, so that their father could attend judicial sessions concerning a spate of robberies. Prince Edward also visited Coventry on a number of occasions. In the Middle Ages this was the largest town in the Midlands, and Edward's position as Earl of Chester meant he was one of the lords of the city, enjoying a special relationship with it. His first visit came on 28 April 1474, when he was welcomed at the Bablake Gate by the City Corporation who presented him with a gift of a 15 ounce gilt cup and then staged a pageant for him that featured locals dressed as 'three kings of Cologne', whose presence served to stress the antiquity of the House of Luxembourg, the royal house from which Edward's mother was descended. 'Welcome, full high and noble prince,' the balladeers proclaimed,

> to this your chamber, so called of antiquity! The presence of your noble person rejoices all our hearts. We must bless the time of your nativity. The right line of the royal line is now as it should be, wherefore God of his goodness preserve you in bodily health, to us and all your tenants here, perpetual joy, and wealth to all the land.

The mayor and the corporation then swore allegiance and Edward stood godfather to the mayor's son. At a later time Prince Edward was involved in arbitrating disputes between some Coventry priors and dissident local figures, two of whom were imprisoned briefly in Ludlow castle.

London also featured regularly on the prince's itinerary. In addition to the frequent formal visits to the Palace of Westminster, which have already been discussed, Christmas often saw Edward attend a family gathering in one of the royal residences just outside the capital, for instance Windsor Castle in 1481 and Eltham Palace the following year. The latter – in royal hands since 1305, when the Bishop of Durham had gifted it to Edward II – was, in Edward Plantagenet's day, situated amid royal hunting grounds in Kent, though it has long since been swallowed up by London's humdrum southeasterly spread. Edward IV liked Eltham Palace and in the 1470s commissioned the construction of its great hall (still standing, and still impressive, despite being used as barn in the nineteenth century). Here, in 1482, some 2,000 people sat down to a great Christmas feast, Prince Edward among them. His father must have been proud to show off the newly built hall to his sons (then aged 12 and 9) and the assembled nobles. It seems entirely probable that this occasion was the last time that Edward met with either of his parents; four months later his dead father was being buried at St George's Chapel, Windsor, while his mother was in sanctuary in Westminster Abbey, fearing for her future as Richard of Gloucester took Edward into his custody.

When the Christmas festivities in London, Eltham or Windsor were over, Edward was usually back on the road to Ludlow by the New Year, and his formal gift (or 'largesse') of £3 paid to the Heralds at Westminster every 1 January was often presented in absentia. Ludlow was not on any main through-routes (and remains so today), making the start and end of each of these journeys, along the lesser-used border road that linked Hereford and Shrewsbury via Ludlow, rather difficult and slow. The more northerly of the two routes that could be taken was along Watling Street, which linked Shrewsbury and London via Lichfield, Coventry, Towcester, Dunstable and St Albans, while to the south Hereford lay on the main road linking London and South Wales via Gloucester, Witney, Oxford and High Wycombe. The journey time between Ludlow and London along either route would have been around a week – longer if winter rains had rendered the roads muddy and difficult to pass.

Two final places in the Marches that Edward Plantagenet probably visited are worth commenting on here. One was the great priory church dedicated to St Milburga at Much Wenlock, some 16 miles northeast of Ludlow (though a substantial knuckle in the landscape separating the two towns, known as Wenlock Edge, would mean a journey there would likely take a roundabout route via Shrewsbury). The small town, of narrow streets and half-timbered buildings, had grown up around the great priory, which Roger de Montgomery (the builder of the castle and abbey in nearby Shrewsbury) had founded in the late eleventh century on the site of an Anglo Saxon monastery. The priory church was the site of a shrine to Milburga, the daughter of a king of Mercia, and a former abbess of the priory; she died around 715, and her bones, previously thought lost, were rediscovered in 1101 by the monks whom Roger had introduced from France the previous decade. In Edward Plantagenet's time the grand monastic complex, abbey and shrine comprised one of the great places of pilgrimage in England; dissolution inevitably came the following century, since when the place has been in ruins – but what substantial ruins they are, with the abbey walls reaching to three storeys and rows of arches and arcades that resolutely remain standing, separated by carefully-tended lawns (courtesy of English Heritage) where the floors of the monastery buildings once lay. In fact there's enough still standing at the former Priory for us to imagine the grand welcome and opulent hospitality that would have been lavished on Edward Plantagenet and his entourage as they came here to feast and pray.

The ruins of the former St Milburga Priory, near Shrewsbury, which Edward Plantagenet probably visited from Ludlow.

Another view of the ruins of the former St Milburga Priory.

Finally, as Edward grew older and became more involved in state business, a place to set aside the concerns of politics – to hunt and relax, too – was required, and Edward's father had Tickenhill Manor in the Wyre Forest town of Bewdley, on the River Severn some 18 miles to the east of Ludlow, styled as a holiday retreat of sorts for the boy. Like Ludlow Castle the manor had been a Mortimer holding, the gift of William the Conqueror to Ralph de Mortimer, Edward's distant ancestor; but it came back into royal possession in the twelfth century, after which it was rebuilt a number of times. Its current appearance dates from a substantial reconstruction in the 1730s, when much of the existing property was demolished, though some work from medieval times remains, including the building's Great Hall. Today the manor house is in private hands, though it occasionally opens its opulent and extensive gardens to visitors.

Ludlow's 'other prince': the castle in Tudor times, and beyond

In May 1499, some two decades after Edward Plantagenet was making regular visits to Tickenhill Manor, the house played host to an extraordinary wedding.

It is difficult to call the pair involved 'the lucky couple'. Arthur Tudor, Prince of Wales, and the presumed heir to his father, King Henry VII, was just 13 years old; his bride, Catherine of Aragon, the daughter of King Ferdinand and Queen Isabella of Spain, was a little younger. (She also wasn't actually present. This was a 'proxy' wedding, with one of the parties absent; somewhat comically the portly Spanish Ambassador Rodrigo de Puebla stood in for the infanta, and it was to be another two years before Catherine finally came face-to-face with Arthur.) Arthur was the offspring of Henry Tudor, the Lancastrian slayer of King Richard III at Bosworth Field, and his wife Elizabeth, the elder sister of the Princes in the Tower. Their union was intended as a sign that Lancaster and York were now at peace; Henry's claim to the English throne had been so tenuous that he had actually commissioned researchers to prove that he was descended from England's great mythical king, and now his son had been named Arthur to convince the country's war-shattered nobility of his credentials as a future English monarch. Moreover, Arthur had been born in Winchester – considered in the Middle Ages to be the site of Camelot – to leave no doubt that a new, strong Arthurian England would arise after the catastrophe of the Wars of the Roses. (Arthur's baptism at Winchester Cathedral, conducted by Bishop Alcock, must have been vested with mystical as well as Christian significance.)

But the rising of a new Arthurian England was not to be. After the proxy wedding at Tickenhill and an 'actual' wedding at St Paul's Cathedral in London two years later, Arthur and his new bride took up residence at Ludlow Castle. Arthur knew the place well; he had been sent there at the age of 6 in 1493, to be schooled in knightly conduct as Edward Plantagenet had been twenty years before. The castle was partly rebuilt for Arthur and his new bride (their rooms were probably located on the upper floors of Roger Mortimer's solar block); but within a few months Arthur was dead from a mysterious illness, leaving his parents' hopes dashed and Catherine, little more than a child, a widow. On 23 April 1502, three weeks after his death, Arthur's body was ceremonially carried from Ludlow Castle to St Laurence's Parish Church, where – as we have seen – his heart was buried. Then began the long journey, via a night when the coffin rested at Tickenhill, across the Clee Hills and through the Wyre Forest to Worcester Cathedral, where Arthur was laid to rest in a splendid tomb that can still be seen to this day.

Henry VII had brought up his sons in the same manner as his forebear Edward IV, at least in terms of geography; the older one, his intended heir, spent his boyhood enjoying the hills and hunting grounds around Ludlow, while his younger son, Prince Henry, stayed closer to home at Eltham Palace. On Arthur's death Henry became the heir presumptive, and on his accession to the throne as Henry VIII he married Catherine of Aragon, his brother's widow. She was later to state that her marriage to Arthur had never been consummated, which (according to some lawyers) meant that Henry could divorce her and marry Anne Boleyn without obtaining special dispensation from the Pope. As everyone knows, though, in the end Henry was forced to divorce Catherine by breaking with Rome and becoming head of his own church – but that's a story that has been told plenty of times before.

Of the two Princes of Wales brought up in Ludlow, Arthur is vastly more celebrated; the Romantic hero who married a Spanish Princess and died tragically young, his story lacks the darkness of Edward Plantagenet's (and there's a tomb, too, which helps in the popularisation of his story). Today there are items for sale in Ludlow Castle's gift shop emblazoned with Prince Arthur's image, while the castle's role as the home of Edward Plantagenet is much less prominent (and often wrongly described too; plenty of 'literature' available in Ludlow Castle states that Edward and Richard, the 'little princes in the Tower', were brought up here together, but Richard was of course brought up in London and probably only came to Ludlow once in his life, just a few days after his birth). And Ludlow's royal connections died with Arthur. None of his successors were sent to grow up here. Henry VIII chose to keep his sickly heir, the future Edward VI, close to hand in London; no draughty castle in the countryside for his upbringing. Neither of his successors, Edward and his half-sisters Mary and Elizabeth, had any children. But the castle's political role continued during their reigns, as it was here that the Council of Wales and the Marches was based – a body that had its origins in the council Edward IV had established for his infant son in the early 1470s.

Through Tudor and early Stuart times Ludlow Castle remained both the *de facto* capital of Wales and a royal castle. In 1616, it hosted the ceremonies that declared James I's son, the future Charles I, Prince of Wales, an event emblematic of its continued position as a place of extravagance and opulence. Every Christmas the Great Hall, where Edward Plantagenet had celebrated his proclamation as king and Arthur Tudor had danced with his new Spanish bride, was the scene of festivities and merry-making. In 1579 things got out of hand at the feast and the roof caught fire; the grand fireplace, now 'suspended' halfway up the east wall of the hall because of the lack of a floor, dates from the rebuilding that followed. In 1634 the First Earl of Bridgewater came to celebrate his new post at the head of the Council by arranging the very first staging of John Milton's *Comus* in the Hall. This work, by a prolific author whose most famous work nowadays is *Paradise Lost,* was a masque, a courtly entertainment where an allegorical tale was told through a mix of music, dancing, singing, acting and elaborate stage design – an early incarnation of opera. The music on that occasion was by the composer Henry Lawes; Milton's text was later used by another composer, Thomas Arne, for a performance of *Comus* in London in 1738, and in June 1745 George Frederic Handel's version was performed once again in the Great Hall at Ludlow.

By then, although the Great Hall might have been in a fit state to stage an extravagant theatrical performance, much of the rest of the castle was badly neglected. The last great rebuilding work had been carried out under Sir Henry Sidney, President of the Council of the Marches from 1560 to 1586, who like Prince Arthur had his heart buried in St Laurence's Church. His weather-worn coat of arms can still be seen above the entrance to the castle's inner bailey, overlooking the stone bridge that visitors use today to cross the moat. Sir Henry and his immediate successors maintained a grand household in the castle; but in 1641 the Council's judicial powers were removed, and the influence of the President and the Council waned until the body was finally abolished in 1689. This marked the start of the castle's demise. In around 1710 the lead was stripped from the roofs, and the following decade the writer Daniel Defoe was able to describe the castle as 'the very perfection of decay' in his *Tour Through the Whole Island of Great Britain*. 'All the fine courts, the royal apartments, halls, and rooms of state, lie open, abandoned, and some of them falling down,' he wrote;

> for since the Courts of the President and Marches are taken away, here is nothing to do that requires the attendance of any public people; so that time, the great devourer of the works of men, begins to eat into the very stone walls, and spread the face of royal ruins over the whole fabric.

In 1765 Ludlow's MP, the Earl of Powis, cast his eye over what was left of the castle, and took on the lease. He was planning to demolish the building and use the site for a new country residence, but died before the wreckers could move in. After his death the Powis family decided on a different fate for the castle and set about doing the place up, repairing the walls and laying paths around the perimeter that gave a view over the river. The family gained full ownership of the castle in 1811, and it remains in their hands to this day.

Ludlow discovered its Arcadian ambience just as the Powis family began to create a family-friendly destination out of the ruins. Today they run the place with the know-how of English Heritage, which over the years has made the castle visitor-friendly, adding a new floor deck to the Great Hall, installing staircases to take visitors to high vantage points, and scattering the place with handrails, seating and litter bins. There's a visitors' centre in the old Porter's Lodge and a tearoom in the former prison. You can even stay in hotel-style rooms built into the outer curtain walls. On Bank Holidays the castle positively heaves, with jousting tournaments and displays of hawking in the outer bailey, and food sold from stalls by Ludlow townsfolk; scenes that would be familiar – just – to Edward Plantagenet when he was growing up here as a boy, and when, in the fateful month of April 1483, he received devastating news from London that his father was dead and he was now king.

Chapter Three

A Coup on Watling Street –
Northampton and Stony Stratford

When he wooed and later married Elizabeth Woodville near her ancestral home at Grafton, in the heart of England, King Edward IV was the very epitome of rugged masculinity: tall, handsome, athletic and well-built. Twenty years later the picture was very different. Dominic Mancini described how Edward was, by the 1480s, 'most immoderate with food and drink' and that he had degenerated into 'a man of … corpulence, so fond [was he] of boon companionship, vanities, debauchery, extravagance and sensual enjoyment.' Novelists have enjoyed conveying this image in fiction. 'His magnificent body had turned to corpulence and flabbiness,' writes Terence Morgan in *The Master of Bruges*. The king, he recounts, usually spent 'the afternoon and evening drinking so much that he was normally carried to his bed in an unconscious condition by four strong manservants'. On a fishing trip on the Thames in March 1483 Edward – according to the Croyland Chronicle – 'allowed the damp cold to strike his vitals'; within a week he was in bed, perhaps with pneumonia. A stroke followed, and finally did for him. He died on 9 April 1483, at the age of just 40.

This was a time of fierce political rivalry. The death of a king could be an uncertain and dangerous time. Edward's own reign had been marked by him being deposed and then taking back his crown from his usurper. But when he himself died, no one doubted the succession – at least not at first. On King Edward's death the crown passed to his eldest son, Edward Plantagenet, and mud-spattered messengers rode across England to bring the news to Ludlow Castle; the 12-year-old prince was now king. In Emma Darwin's *A Secret Alchemy*, Edward's mother Elizabeth Woodville tries to calm her fears at the news.

He is tall, it is true … but his body is a boy's, lightly built, malleable, his bones yet fragile and his skin still thin. How heavy is the mantle that his father, in dying too soon, cast upon his son's small shoulders? Ned's hands are still so slender that in the sunlight you might fancy you could see the bones beneath the blue veins that thread through his white skin.

Philippa Gregory has Elizabeth thinking the same thoughts in *The White Queen*. 'My boy is not quite thirteen, in God's name…. His voice is still fluting, his chin is smooth as a girl's, he has the softest fair down on his upper lip that you can only see when his face is in profile, against the light.'

As Edward and the higher members of his household set off in grand procession from Ludlow for the coronation in London, his uncle Richard of Gloucester, brother of the dead king, was also on the road. He had set out on his journey south from his great castle at Middleham in the Yorkshire Dales some days previously, and had agreed to meet the new king and his entourage at Northampton. But no one among the king's party was aware that Richard intended to take Edward into his custody, least of all the young king himself, whom history has cast as an innocent pawn caught up in the deadly web of politics that Richard of Gloucester was weaving – and first, he had to get the boy into his hands. This he did at a small town on Watling Street just south of Northampton, named Stony Stratford, which – by chance – was only a short distance from the manor house and forest where his brother Edward had wooed the fair Elizabeth Woodville all those years before.

On the road

As we have seen in the previous chapter, Edward Plantagenet was a frequent traveller and must have known the main roads of the Midlands, South East England and the Welsh Marches well. Travel was more common in medieval England than is popularly supposed. After the decline of the feudal system and the economic ravages wrought by the Black Death in the 1370s, labourers were often compelled to travel around the country in search of work. Their fellow travellers would have included minstrels, merchants, outlaws, traders, messengers, preachers, friars, pilgrims, revenue collectors, travelling justices, bishops – and kings, nobles and princes too, or soldiers serving them. When kings travelled they were accompanied by lengthy baggage trains consisting of carts laden with gold from the royal treasury and clothes from the royal wardrobe; we can assume that this was the form that Edward Plantagenet's party took as its members set off from Ludlow. In previous centuries, Kings John and Edward I in particular seem to have had busy and extensive itineraries around England, and what we know about the condition and network of medieval roads comes partly from them.

Most principal roads in medieval England were former Roman roads. An astonishing 16,000km of roads had been constructed by the Romans by 150AD, but well over a millennium later many of these were in a poor state of repair. In some places the original Roman paving would have survived, in others it would have gone, pilfered for local building schemes or buried beneath blown earth, and a clear way through the countryside would be forged by a track using the old foundations of the road. Where paving remained, travellers would often shun the hard, pitted surface the Romans had laid down for softer ground either side of the road. As a result, many medieval roads were fringed by weaving tracks that ran roughly parallel with the original road; these were eventually abandoned in the seventeenth century, when the common land over which these roads passed was enclosed by landowners, and traffic was confined to the original road once more (these were the roads that became the turnpikes of the eighteenth century). Sometimes these parallel tracks still show up as indentations in the ground surface today, either side of modern roads, and can often be identified using aerial photography.

It is difficult to make judgments about the general state of repair of medieval roads. John Leland, in his *Itineraries*, said nothing about the actual roads on which he travelled to compile his survey, and neither Chaucer nor his Canterbury pilgrims had anything to say about the road that they took from Southwark to Canterbury in *The Canterbury Tales;* so perhaps the quality of the roads was not worth commenting on and better than we might imagine. It is commonly thought that roads were often impassable in winter or during rain, but this was not always so; in January 1300 Edward I covered the distance from Bamburgh in Northumberland to Windsor in twenty-five days, including six days when he did not travel – so his average daily distance was a creditable 20 miles, and this in the depths of a northern winter. Roads would have been repaired by specialist road menders whose work was organised by town corporations and religious houses, and paid for by alms and bequests (as the provision and maintenance of roads was a seen as a pious act). In 1285 Edward I had written to the Prior of Dunstable complaining that Watling Street, where it passed through his town, was 'so broken up and deep by the frequent passage of carts, that dangerous injuries continuously threaten those passing by these roads,' and went on to 'command you ...shall cause these roads to be filled in and mended, as in such case it has been accustomed to be done in times past.' In the same year Edward also set down regulations that land should be cleared for 200ft on either side of major roads so that vagabonds could not hide in undergrowth as they lay in wait for unwary travellers.

The most comprehensive map of medieval roads was the so-called Gough map of 1360, named after Richard Gough, the eighteenth century antiquarian who first described it. It shows just under 3,000 miles of road criss-crossing England – though in some places the lines on the map might have denoted a simple right-of-way rather than a specific trackway through field and forest. The map also shows the four 'royal' ways, which were Watling Street, Ermine Street, the Fosse Way and the Icknield Way. According to tradition all travellers on these roads enjoyed the special privilege of the 'king's peace', which criminalised any assault committed on them; however there's no evidence that royal jurisdiction was confined only to these four roads. Each of these roads is of unguessable age; some stretches might have had their origins as clearings through the forest forged deep in antiquity.

Watling Street was the most important of these roads – indeed it was the artery of medieval Britain. It connected Dover with Holyhead, the Welsh port that lies across the Irish Sea from Dublin, so threading together England, Wales and Ireland. Its first stretch linked the English Channel with Westminster by way of Canterbury. Beyond London, the road passed through St Albans and Towcester, crossing the Fosse Way (which ran from Exeter to Lincoln) at High Cross; it then went through Cannock, Shrewsbury and Chester before traversing North Wales. The route it followed is that taken by the modern-day A2, the A5 and the M6 toll roads. Its presence in the landscape seems as old as time. The thirteenth-century St Albans monk Matthew Paris claimed that the road had been built by the British king Belinus, who ruled in the fourth century BC and whose story (like that of King Arthur) was recounted by the cleric and historian Geoffrey of Monmouth. However, historians now believe the figure of Belinus to be fictional. So was the road created by pre-Roman Celtic tribes as a way of linking far-flung parts of the island? Or was it a series of local routes that just happened to become connected? Its name seems indelibly linked to the Romans, yet they never knew it as Watling Street; to them the road was simply Iter II and Iter III (Iter being Latin for 'route'), part of a pan-European network of roads that could take marching armies from Britain to Rome and beyond. The name of the road comes from later on, during the Dark Ages, when a tribal chieftain named Wæcla governed the territory around St Albans. Little is known of the Wæclingas – the people of Wæcla – but the road went through their territory and they were responsible for it, and somehow the name extended to all the other parts of the road, including far-flung sections in Wales and Kent, a long way from Wæcla's territory. For much of the Dark Ages the road marked the boundary between Saxon England to the west and Viking-ruled Danelaw to the east; by the Middle Ages, when Edward Plantagenet was making frequent journeys along the road – during one of which he was taken into custody by his uncle at an inn that probably fronted onto it – there was no such observable division.

Northampton: a king 'most honourably confined'

Northampton was not on Watling Street. It lay just to the north, on a road from Leicester and Nottingham that joined Watling Street just to the south of the town. Richard of Gloucester and his chief henchman, the Duke of Buckingham, entered the town on 29 April from the north, expecting to rendezvous with Rivers and the king, who were travelling by stages along Watling Street from the northwest. According to the Croyland chronicle Richard had joined forces with Buckingham, who had travelled from his estates at Brecon in South Wales, just north of Northampton. Both had a retinue of armed men with them. The choice of routes taken by all three parties was deliberate; Dominic Mancini reported that Rivers had agreed with a missive of Richard's that 'in their company Edward's entry into the city [London] might be more magnificent', and the plan was that after linking up in Northampton the new king would travel the rest of the way to the capital in the company of Lord Buckingham (who was married to Queen Elizabeth's sister) and both his uncles (Richard of Gloucester and Earl Rivers). This was the reason for the choice of route that Rivers made; the more southerly route from Ludlow to London via Hereford and Oxford was probably shorter, but taking the more northerly route along Watling Street allowed for the intended rendezvous at Northampton. Rivers had agreed to this as he was anxious to quell any rumours of a division besetting the royal council; what he could not have known, however, is what Richard was planning for him at Northampton.

Northampton is a historic town – it was founded by the Danes in 850 after their invasion of Mercia – and though the resolutely modern centre boasts some fine historic buildings, these are mostly from the eighteenth century, by which time the town had become a major centre for footwear and leather manufacturing. The railway station now occupies the position of the once-mighty, long-vanished castle (though a rebuilt entrance portal survives), and the only prominent structures that remain from the Middle Ages are churches. Richard and his entourage would have passed by the most historic of these as they entered the town through the North Gate (of which no trace now survives); this was Simon de Senlis' Church of the Holy Sepulchre, whose round nave is of the same design as the round chapel in Ludlow Castle. On their entry into Northampton, Richard and Buckingham expected to meet with Rivers and the king – but they were nowhere to be seen. On enquiring, Richard discovered that although the king and Rivers had passed through Northampton, they had moved on to Stony Stratford, 14 miles to the south. Rivers later claimed that this was because of the lack of suitable accommodation in Northampton; but it has been suggested that Sir Richard Grey, Edward Plantagenet's half-brother, had ridden up Watling Street from London with a message from the queen that Richard's intentions might be suspect, and that the royal party should abandon their plan of linking up with him and instead push on towards London. Whatever the situation, Richard and Buckingham had no problem finding accommodation in Northampton, and took rooms in three neighbouring inns, Richard and his party in one, and Buckingham in another. Tradition suggests that Richard's inn was the Talbot Inn on the Market Square, which, in the manner of inns of the day, was probably a poky place of long wooden corridors and dingy rooms. There is no way of confirming this, however, and the inn burned down in 1685, leaving no trace behind – even its precise location is a matter of conjecture. Desmond Seward's 1982 biography of Richard III claims the Talbot Inn was not on the Market Square but was situated at 81–3 High Street; if we assume that this is Addington Street, the name for Northampton's High Street, then this address is now a nondescript modern building housing the offices of a building society. All of this is a shame, as for around twenty-four hours this inn became the centre of operations for Richard's audacious coup against the Woodvilles, the political ground zero for what was arguably the most astonishing usurpation of power in English history.

At first Richard's approach to Rivers and Grey was amicable, even jovial. The two men were fetched from Stony Stratford (leaving the young king with Bishop Alcock) and were given the third of the inns commandeered by Richard in Northampton. Their conduct had not been creditable; a rendezvous had, after all, been arranged and agreed by all of them, and whatever the accommodation situation in Northampton, Rivers and his party should have waited there for Richard and Buckingham, rather than pressing on along the road. Yet Richard, apparently magnanimous in the face of this sleight, 'graciously received' Rivers and Grey at Northampton, according to Dominic Mancini. Thomas More goes further: 'There was made that night much friendly cheer between these two dukes and Lord Rivers,' he recounts, and the men spent 'a great part of the night in conviviality'. More goes on to say that once Rivers and Grey had retired to their inn, Buckingham and Richard, along with Richard Ratcliffe, another of Richard's retainers, then talked long into the night. Another important chronicler of these events, Polydore Vergil, a cleric from Urbino, Italy, who lived in England from 1501 and whose *Anglia Historia* (History of England) was commissioned by Henry VII, maintains that it was during this late-night session in the inn – which probably went on until morning – that Richard told Buckingham his intent to usurp the Kingdom. Whatever the precise nature of the febrile conversation in the inn that night, it is clear that at dawn Rivers and Grey found their lodgings surrounded by Richard's armed soldiers. According to Mancini the two men came on the receiving end of an angry barrage of accusations from Richard, which centred on his rights as Lord Protector being denied. The men were placed in the charge of Sir Thomas Gower, another of Richard's trusted henchmen, while Richard and Buckingham took their horses and galloped south to Stony Stratford, to take charge of King Edward as he prepared to head on towards London.

Back in Northampton later that day, their royal quarry now delivered into their hands, Richard and Buckingham sat down to a celebratory meal in their inn, while Rivers and Grey languished in separate rooms in the third inn. The young king also had a room to himself, and all three were securely guarded. As the meal progressed 'the Duke of Glouester sent a dish from his own table to the Lord Rivers, praying him to be of good cheer, all should be well enough', Thomas More wrote; but Rivers didn't touch his meal, and asked for it to be given to Grey. After dinner Richard wrote to the Lord Mayor of London, Sir Edmund Shaa (or Shaw), explaining what he had done. He had 'not confined his nephew the King of England,' he clarified, 'rather, had rescued him and the realm from perdition, since the young man would have fallen into the hands of those who, since they had not spared either the honour or life of the father, could not be expected to have more regard for the youthfulness of the son.' No one, Richard made it clear, had such solicitude for the welfare of King Edward and the preservation of the state as he did. And he informed Shaa that he and the boy would be in London within a few days so that 'the Coronation might be more splendidly performed'. Was King Edward a prisoner? Or was he being kept safe from his enemies? Dominic Mancini maintains that throughout that night Richard and Buckingham took turns at guarding him, 'for they were afraid lest he should escape or be forcibly delivered from their hands.' Richard's detractors would claim that his actions in Stony Stratford and Northampton were illegal and that the arrests and later executions of Rivers and Grey were acts of tyranny; his supporters would counter such claims by maintaining that the Woodvilles had acted precipitously and had staged a coup of their own against Richard. What is certainly clear is that on that day England was plunged into a political crisis whose culmination – according to popular tradition, at any rate – was the murder of two innocent boys in the Tower of London.

Stony Stratford

Stony Stratford is a town on the road. Its name suggests as much: it's where the street – from the Latin 'stretten' – fords a river, in this case the Ouse; the 'Stony' part of the name suggests that the bed of the river consisted of stones at this point. Originally a skinny settlement strung out along Watling Street, today the town centre is entirely focused on the road, which cuts through it in an arrow-straight trajectory; heading southeast, it's 50 miles to London, while to the northwest the road cuts between Coventry and Leicester as it curves its way through the northern part of the West Midlands. Mundane shops now occupy buildings that once housed wayside inns for those travelling along the road. In their *Murray's Buckinghamshire Architectural Guide* of 1948, John Betjeman and John Piper described how the town boasted 'some fine Georgian brick houses and later shop fronts [that lined] each side of thundering Watling street,' before going on to comment laconically on the vaulting in the parish church. The traffic no longer thunders along Watling Street – through traffic bypasses the town – and though it appears to be a small country town, Stony Stratford is today part of the Borough of Milton Keynes, whose central station is only twenty minutes away on the bus (the journey allows passengers views of the roundabouts, concrete cows and windswept plazas for which the 1960s New Town is famous). So thanks to boundary changes, this Buckinghamshire market town is now part of the biggest experiment in urban planning ever conducted in Britain. Slightly dismissive of the famous New Town in its midst, Stony Stratford calls itself on its website 'The Jewel of Milton Keynes'.

The High Street in Stony Stratford is actually a part of Watling Street.

While the location of the inn in Northampton where Richard planned and concluded his coup is now lost to history, in Stony Stratford things seem – at first sight – to be more certain. A building (now a private house) that once housed the Rose and Crown inn still stands fronting Watling Street (named simply the High Street at this point), its muted pastel-pink façade somewhat peeling now. On the exterior wall is a maroon plaque, framed by the ensigns of a white rose (for the House of York) and a crown, a neat allusion to both the inn's name and the events that supposedly unfolded here. 'This house,' the plaque maintains, 'was anciently the Rose and Crown Inn and here in 1483 Richard, Duke of Gloucester (Richard III) captured the uncrowned boy King Edward V, who was later murdered in the Tower of London.' However, the reality is far less clear-cut. The Rose and Crown was a small inn whose building and foundation date from Tudor times; it is by no means certain that an inn actually occupied this site in 1483, still less that it was called the Rose and Crown. In 1735 the antiquarian Browne Willis suggested that it was more likely

The former Rose and Crown Inn in Stony Stratford, whose frontage opens out onto Watling Street. According to tradition it was outside this inn that Richard Duke of Gloucester took the boy-King Edward V into his custody.

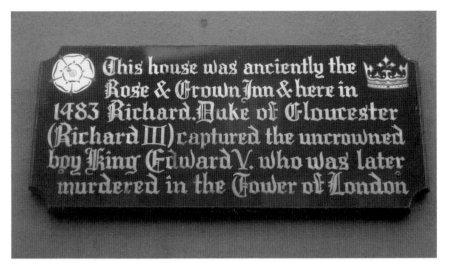

This house was anciently the Rose & Crown Inn & here in 1483 Richard.Duke of Gloucester (Richard III) captured the uncrowned boy King Edward V. who was later murdered in the Tower of London

Plaque on the exterior of the Rose and Crown Inn that recalls the events of 1483.

that Edward and the principal members of his party had stayed at the much larger Swan Inn, which in the Middle Ages occupied 92–4 High Street (the property has been completely rebuilt several times since). But really, nothing is known for certain beyond the fact that Edward V did reside in the town for a night; the notion that he stayed at the Rose and Crown probably dates to the early nineteenth century, when there was an upsurge in interest in local history – though why this inn was chosen as the 'actual' one in which Edward stayed is difficult to determine.

So the precise inn that Earl Rivers had commandeered for the night for himself and his young charge on 30 April 1483 remains unknown. But for a few minutes the next morning, the inn (or more probably its courtyard or its street-facing exterior) became the setting for an extraordinary and epoch-making drama, the repercussions of which were to last generations. With Earl Rivers safely under arrest in Northampton, Richard 'with a large body of soldiers, and in company with the Duke of Buckingham … hastened at full gallop towards the young king at Stony Stratford,' taking Sir Richard Grey with them. When they reached Stony Stratford they found Edward already mounted on his horse outside the inn, alongside Vaughan, ready to leave. They were waiting for Rivers to get back from Northampton so that they could push on towards London. Instead the approaching figures on horseback turned out to be Richard and Buckingham, who, as Mancini continues, 'saluted [Edward] as their sovereign'. Thomas More claims that

Edward received the two men 'in very joyous and amiable manner', while the Croyland chronicle maintains that Richard 'did not omit or refuse to pay every mark of respect to the king his nephew, in the way of uncovering his head, bending the knee, or other posture required of a subject.' According to Mancini, Richard and Buckingham then proceeded to explain why there were there, and why they hadn't brought Grey and Rivers with them. The ministers that served the new king's father, they claimed, 'had ruined his health ... wherefore [carried on Buckingham] lest these same ministers should play the same old game with the son [they] should be removed from the king's side, because such a child would be incapable of governing so great a realm by means of puny men.' Richard added that those self-same ministers were conspiring to kill him and had prepared ambushes in the capital, and that he, Richard, was much better placed to discharge the duties of government, owing to his experience and popularity. He then broke the news to Edward that Earl Rivers and Richard Grey had been arrested at Northampton.

Edward – who listened to all this mounted on his horse – was sceptical of what the two men had told him. According to Mancini he told Richard that 'he merely had those ministers whom his father had given him and, relying on his father's prudence, he believed that good and faithful ones had been given him. He could see no evil in them and wished to keep them.' These words of Edward, recorded by Mancini and More, constitute the only recorded occasion on which the boy made a personal contribution to the unfolding events at which he was at the centre; according to the former, the young king possessed 'the likeness of his father's noble spirit' as he spoke. 'What my brother marquess has done I cannot say,' More records Edward saying in response to Richard's accusation that Sir Thomas Grey had been helping himself from the royal treasury. But the boy nonetheless vouched for the innocence of Rivers and Grey, and stated that he 'had great confidence in the peers of the realm and the queen'. The mention of the queen's name met with a furious riposte from Buckingham, who maintained that 'it was not the business of women but of men to govern kingdoms, and so if [Edward] cherished any confidence in her he had better relinquish it'. Instead the boy should place 'all his hope in his barons [he meant himself and Richard], who excelled in power and nobility.'

That was the cue for the hammer to fall. The discussions and cajoling were over. 'They arrested Grey, Vaughan [Edward's chamberlain] and

Haute [the controller of his household] in the King's presence,' says Mancini, 'and handed them over to the care of guards ... [Edward] surrendered himself to the care of his uncle, which was inevitable, for although the dukes cajoled him by moderation, yet they clearly showed that they were demanding rather than supplicating.' Mancini went on to say that the other members of the king's party were compelled to withdraw, and 'not approach any place to which the king might chance to come, under penalty of death'. One leading figure of Edward's party was, however, spared arrest; the Tudor chronicler John Rous records that Edward's 'special tutor and diligent mentor in goodly ways, Master John Alcock' was 'removed like all the rest but not, however, subject to the rigours of imprisonment.' Naturally, the whole affair distressed the young boy who, traumatised and isolated, 'wept and was nothing content,' according to Thomas More. 'But it booted [mattered] not' as, in Rous's words, the young king 'was received like an innocent lamb into the hands of wolves.'

Shakespeare does not portray these events in his play *Richard III*. In fact he actively plays fast and loose with history, having Richard and Buckingham set off to intercept the king's party from London rather than from Middleham and Brecon. In Act II Scene II, Buckingham conspires with Richard and suggests that 'whoever journeys to the Prince / For God's sake, let not us two be behind. For, by the way, I'll sort occasion.... To part the queen's proud kindred [i.e. Lord Rivers] from the king.' Then in Scene IV of the same act, the Archbishop of York outlines the progress of the king's party to Queen Elizabeth, who is at Westminster with her youngest son, Richard. 'Last night, I hear, they lay at Stony Stratford / And at Northampton they do rest tonight,' he tells her. 'Tomorrow or next day they will be here [London].' Later on a messenger announces that 'Lord Rivers and Lord Grey are sent to Pomfret [Pontefract] and with them Sir Thomas Vaughan, prisoners' – to which Elizabeth cries that she sees 'the ruin of my house, the tiger hath now seized the gentle hind ... I see, as in a map, the end of all'. With that she heads off to the sanctuary of Westminster Abbey with her younger son.

While Shakespeare covers the momentous events that unfolded at Stony Stratford by simply reporting them, other dramatisations of the story of the princes actually overlook the Stony Stratford episode entirely. One is the 1962 film *Tower of London*, directed in stylish black-and-white by cult horror-mystery maestro Roger Corman. The film – campy by today's standards, though it has acquired cult status over the years – was inspired (though is not a remake) of a 1939 film of the same title (regular horror star Vincent Price played the Duke of Clarence in the earlier film, and played Richard III in the second). Corman's film, full of shimmering ghosts and gloomy shadows, borrows many elements from Shakespeare's *Richard III*, though it gives the chronology of the story a hefty shuffle; Edward Plantagenet (who mysteriously sports an American accent in the film) never actually leaves London – so there is no need to include any scenes in which Richard of Gloucester takes him prisoner in an English market town. Richard Loncraine's 1995 film *Richard III* is a much different version of the story, presenting its anti-hero (played by Ian Mckellen) as a 1930s dictator, though managing to utilise much of Shakespeare's original dialogue. In Loncraine's film Prince Edward is seen arriving in London in great pomp and style on the royal train soon after his father's death, met by his over-excited younger brother (who is very interested in the train) and falling into Richard of Gloucester's hands (and the Tower's clutches) soon after – much as in Shakespeare's play.

Novelists – as opposed to film-makers – have seemed much happier with presenting the events in Stony Stratford as they actually unfolded, and have realised that the ingredients for a scene of dramatic potency are almost unmatched; an innocent young boy whom fate has thrust into the limelight too early, locked in an unequal battle of wills with English history's favourite pantomime villain; the country's political future at stake; the whole thing played out against the comparatively ordinary background of a small roadside town in the Midlands. In her novel *The Seventh Son* Reay Tannahill describes Edward as 'a goodlooking lad' as he sat on his horse outside the Stony Stratford inn,

> tall for his age – almost as tall as Richard – and angelically fair, though there was a touch of ice and arrogance about him … [he wore] a high-buttoned, knee-length purple velvet gown, with its bagpipe sleeves swelling out from the wrists to form hanging pouches or pockets [and a] purple velvet bonnet with its narrow turned-up brim perched on his short fair curls.

Her novel is sympathetic to Richard, who seems wronged at every turn. Inevitably, then, his adversary at Stony Stratford is described as a jumped-up spoiled brat. 'The boy was already in the courtyard [of the inn] with three or four members of his household, preparing to set out' when Richard and Buckingham arrived. The two men reined in 'with a dramatic flourish ... leapt from their horses, bared their heads, and bent their knees in the approved fashion.' Tannahill uses some of the dialogue recorded by More and others in the scene that follows; when Richard finally persuades Edward to go with him, 'the boy's lips quivered', but he walks with dignity through the courtyard and out onto Watling Street, where his grooms help him to mount his horse. 'If he had been quick ... he could have galloped off to seek the protection of his armed escort, but perhaps dignity forbade, or perhaps he was just afraid,' she concludes. (How's that scenario for one of history's greatest 'what if' musings?)

Philippa Gregory sees the same scene differently. In *The White Queen* she describes what Edward's mother feels after she has been told of the events in Stony Stratford.

> He is only a boy.... He has to stand up to a battle-hardened man who is determined to do wrong. He says that he is certain that his uncle Anthony is a good man and a fine guardian ... he does not know how to stand up to his uncle Richard, dressed in black and with a face like thunder, two thousand men in his train and ready to fight ... he cries bitterly. They tell me that. He cries like a child when no one will obey him.

Interestingly, the way this scene plays out in the television adaptation of this novel is faithful neither to the original novel nor to history. The 'capturing' of Edward takes place in a forest (rather than outside an inn in a town) after a sword fight (there's no record that one took place), and features a rather glacial Edward (black haired and played by a child actor rather older than 12) who afterwards is taken straight to the Tower of London where his door is personally locked by Richard (with an evil glint in his eye); and then Earl Rivers is arrested not at Northampton but in London, while seeing Edward IV's former whore, Elizabeth Shore. He is then executed at the Tower of London (rather than Pontefract Castle) with both princes looking on, the signal to the executioner given by Richard himself. The sequence clearly borrows elements of the execution of another of Edward's supporters, Lord Hastings, who was also a notorious visitor to the bed of Elizabeth Shore and whose execution at the Tower was possibly witnessed by the imprisoned Edward (but not his younger brother). All in all it's history repackaged wholesale for the Sunday evening TV audience, who should perhaps be treated to something rather better.

Hornsey Park and London

Richard and his young charge – Lord Protector and king – left Northampton on the morning of 3 May, heading southeast along Watling Street, past the inn in Stony Stratford where Edward had stayed with his uncle, and on towards London. Through Bletchley and Dunstable they journeyed, more towns on the road, the Protector 'garbed in black cloth, like a mourner,' wrote Mancini, and 'accompanied by no more than five hundred soldiers'. They made good progress. By evening they had travelled forty 40 miles and had reached St Albans, which was where Edward might have appended his signature to a scrap of parchment that is now preserved in the Cotton Manuscripts collection in the British Library: 'Edwardus Quintus,' his signature reads, his first (or at least the earliest surviving) as king. Richard and Buckingham have also signed the document: 'Loyaultié me lie. Richard Gloucestre'. 'Souvente me souvene. Harre [Harry] Bokynham.'

The following day Edward was welcomed into London at a place known variously as Hornsey Park, Hornsey Great Park or Harringay Park. The chronicle written during the reign of Henry VIII by the lawyer, MP and historian Edward Hall tells us that 'When the king approached the city, Edmund Shaw, goldsmith, then Mayor of the city, with the Aldermen and sheriffs in scarlet, and five hundred commoners ... received his grace reverently at Hornsey Park, and so conveyed him to the city.' In those days Hornsey was a hamlet set among woods and fields some 6 miles north of Charing Cross; today it's firmly part of London's northerly residential spread, a district of the Borough of Haringey and designated by the N8 postcode. The Great Park consisted of the hunting grounds that surrounded a long-vanished palatial residence originally built for the Bishops of London, which had by the 1480s come into Richard's ownership (and was in a slightly different location to the current residential district known as Hornsey Park). It has a history as a gathering place; in 1386 an earlier Duke of Gloucester, accompanied by the Earls of Warwick, Arundel, and other nobles, had assembled here to oppose King Richard II and to compel him to dismiss his two favoured ministers, while Henry VII was escorted into the capital from here after his victory at the Battle of Bosworth. Hornsey is set well to the east of the old course of Watling Street, which entered the capital from the northwest following the route of what is now Edgware Road and Kilburn High Road. The diversion made by the royal party was likely made because of Richard's links with Hornsey and in acknowledgement of its traditional role as a gathering place just outside the capital.

After the reception at Hornsey Edward, riding dressed 'in blue velvet' according to the Great Chronicle of London, was escorted into the capital alongside his uncle, who continuously decried 'Behold your prince and sovereign lord' as they passed by the assembled crowds. Their first destination was the Palace of the Bishop of London, which stood on the site of the present Chapter House beside St Paul's Cathedral (the palace was destroyed in 1650 and today there are no visible remains of it). This palace was occasionally used as a residence by the monarch, and was chosen on this instance as it was both secure – Richard suspected that the Woodvilles might try to orchestrate a counter-coup against his him – and relatively public; Richard had no wish to make people suspect that he was hiding the young king away. Yet this location meant he could also keep an eye on Edward from his redoubt at Baynard's Castle, a great medieval palace on the Thames just 200 metres away (again, no trace remains of this building, which was destroyed during the Great Fire of London; its location is marked today by Castle Baynard street, which runs east from Blackfriars Station, one of London's smaller mainline train termini). Edward's stay at the Bishop's Palace also brought him back onto Watling Street, which crossed the Thames via London Bridge, and ran immediately north of St Paul's Cathedral along what is now Newgate Street and Cheapside. A road leading to the cathedral from the east still carries the name of Watling Street to this day.

Back to Northamptonshire: the great manor house at Grafton

By coincidence Stony Stratford and Northampton play another role in the story of the princes. A completely different one, in fact, that revolves around Grafton, a substantial village 8 miles south of Northampton that straddles the road between the two towns. This village was the seat of Elizabeth Woodville, the princes' mother. (Her name lives on today in the Elizabeth Woodville Secondary School, situated a mile from Stony Stratford.) In the late Middle Ages the Woodville's manor house was by far Grafton's largest building (it was later enlarged by Henry VIII for use as a summer palace, hence the occasional appendage 'Regis' to the name of the village; a farm now occupies the site, though the manor house's floors and foundations were subject to archeological excavations in the 1960s). The Woodvilles were minor gentry. Their lineage stretched back to a Norman knight named William de Wydville. Elizabeth's mother, Jacquetta of Luxembourg, was descended from Charlemagne and, less distantly, from Eleanor Plantagenet, the sister of King Henry III (so the princes inherited Plantagenet blood from both parents). Some of the early action in Emma Darwin's *A Secret Alchemy* and – more particularly – Philippa Gregory's *The White Queen* unfold hereabouts, drawing on the legend that the young King Edward wooed Elizabeth in nearby Whittlebury Forest. Elizabeth then was a widow; her husband, Sir John Grey of Groby, had been killed at the battle of Towton. He had fought for the Lancastrian side, not an auspicious background to his former wife cultivating a romance with a Yorkist king.

When Elizabeth first encountered King Edward he was legendarily intelligent, witty, courageous and handsome – and tall (his skeleton uncovered in 1789 shows he was just over 6ft 3in), the very picture of majesty. Dominic Mancini recorded how, in Whittleberry Forest, Elizabeth had initially resisted Edward's advances; but then came a private (many would say secret) marriage on May Day 1464, probably in the Woodville's private chapel in Grafton, where the only ones present (according to Robert Fabian in his *New Chronicles of England and France*) besides the bride and groom were Elizabeth's mother, a priest, two gentlewomen, and a young man 'to help the priest sing'. Fabian recorded that 'after which spousals ended, [Edward] went to bed [with her], and so tarried there upon three or four hours, and after departed to Stony Stratford', where he told his party he had been away hunting; a day or two later he returned to Grafton and stayed with Elizabeth in secret for three or four days. (There is of course much material here for the writer of popular historical novels: love-making as the light streams through the leaves of the trees; the stays in the idyllic, moated manor-house of Grafton; magnificent steeds riding through thick forests. In the television adaptation of *The White Queen* the king, looking rather too well-scrubbed, exclaims 'I'm mad for you – I've been thinking about you all day long' during one of their sylvan trysts; 'Shouldn't you be thinking about your battle?' Elizabeth replies.)

Elizabeth's marriage plays a vital part in the story of the princes in two ways. Firstly, the power struggle in which the boys were caught up was one that was essentially anti-Woodville, a protest against this parvenu family that had risen far beyond its station (English monarchs usually chose foreign princesses as their wives, and Elizabeth was the first English-born royal consort since the eleventh century). Secondly, when they married, King Edward might already have been married – something that will be discussed later – making Prince Edward and his younger brother illegitimate and therefore unable (Richard of Gloucester claimed) to inherit the throne. To make it worse, Elizabeth's mother Jacquetta was considered by many to be some sort of witch or sorceress. In the Middle Ages, witchcraft allowed intelligent minds to bring potentially damaging charges against opponents; in this case, accusations flowed that Jacquetta had used her sorcery to make King Edward turn his back on the political and financial benefits of a foreign marriage, and marry her daughter instead. In *The White Queen* Philippa Gregory alludes to Jacquetta's magic by maintaining that her and her daughter are descended from a water goddess; when Elizabeth throws threaded charms into the Thames in 1469 she pulls one out and finds that 'at the end is a silver spoon, a beautiful little silver spoon for a baby, and when I catch it in my hand I see, shining in the moonlight, that it is engraved with a coronet and the name "Edward"'. Unfortunately, the water goddess was not at hand some thirteen years later, when young Edward fell into Richard of Gloucester's hands just a few miles from the place where Elizabeth herself had been brought up.

Chapter Four

Palace and Prison: The Tower of London

In the 1070s, when William the Conqueror's great stone fortress began to rise on the north bank of the Thames to the east of London, nothing like it had ever been seen before in England. Designed as a fortress to protect London against seaborne invasions, the Tower also served to overawe Londoners and to provide them with a constant reminder of the permanence and supremacy of the new political order. According to William's first biographer, William of Poitiers, the Conqueror regarded that his first task after his coronation was to 'bring Londoners completely to heel'. Thus the construction of the massive square keep that forms the oldest part of the Tower. Its whitewashed walls and four corner turrets, each rising to a distinctive domed roof, makes this building – the 'White Tower' – one of the most instantly recognisable in the world, familiar even to those who have never even set eyes on it. Completed by 1100 using building stone from William's native Normandy, when it was finished it must have dominated the flat, marshy landscape for miles around. Subsequent centuries have seen massive curtain walls, crenellated defensive towers, a residential palace, domestic ranges, military barracks and a chapel built around the White Tower, which nonetheless remains at the heart of the Tower of London and the most dominant building in the complex.

Throughout its long history the Tower has served several purposes. Its primary function has always been as a fortress and a stronghold, a role that it retains today as the home of the crown jewels. It has also been a prison and a royal palace; for many centuries England's coinage was minted within its walls, and its famous menagerie, which dates from the Holy Roman Emperor Frederick III's gift of three leopards to King Henry III in the year 1210, is the origin of London Zoo and in medieval times provided a popular attraction for Londoners. In 1598 the historian and antiquarian John Stow was able to describe the Tower in his *Survey of London* as:

> a citadel to defend or command the city; a royal palace for assemblies or treaties; a prison of state for the most dangerous offenders; the only place of coinage for all England at this time; the armoury for warlike provision; the treasury of the ornaments and jewels of the crown; and the general conserver of the most records of the king's courts of justice at Westminster.

The Tower retained its military role until the Second World War, during which time it had a designated role to play in the defence of London in the event of a German invasion; today its military role is symbolic (though many of the beefeaters formerly served in the armed forces) and the Tower's principal role is as a tourist attraction, welcoming over 2 million visitors a year. They get to walk through an assemblage of buildings that date from ten centuries, from William's original White Tower (now home to the collections of the royal armouries, a nod to the fact that this building has always been used as a military storehouse) through to the nineteenth century red-brick barrack blocks that flank the White Tower's northern and eastern sides and which now serve as military museums.

The Tower has served as a prison and a place of execution for virtually all of its life. The first prisoner incarcerated here was Ranulf Flambard, Bishop of Durham and chief tax-gatherer for William II, who was imprisoned for extortion in 1100 by William's successor, Henry I (and who managed to escape by befuddling his guards with wine at a banquet, and climbing down from the White Tower using a rope that he had hidden in the wine barrel). In 1941 Rudolf Hess, Hitler's deputy, was held in the Tower after his extraordinary attempt to fly to Scotland and open peace talks with Britain, and in August of the same year the Tower's last execution, of a German spy named Josef Jakobs, was carried out by firing squad in the now-demolished rifle range behind one of the barracks blocks (during the First World War, the Tower witness the execution of eleven men, all shot for espionage). The prisoner that most visitors want to hear about is Anne Boleyn, who was held not in a dungeon or gloomy Tower (as many probably suspect) but in the so-called Queen's House, which Henry VIII had constructed for her in happier circumstances in the 1530s. Half a century before Anne's incarceration and execution the

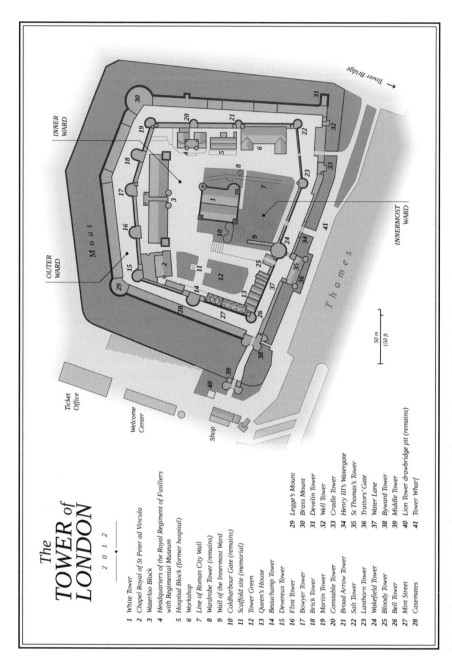

The
TOWER of
LONDON
2 0 1 2

1 White Tower
2 Chapel Royal of St Peter ad Vincula
3 Waterloo Block
4 Headquarters of the Royal Regiment of Fusiliers
with Regimental Museum
5 Hospital Block (former hospital)
6 Workshop
7 Line of Roman City Wall
8 Wardrobe Tower (remains)
9 Wall of the Innermost Ward
10 Coldharbour Gate (remains)
11 Scaffold site (memorial)
12 Tower Green
13 Queen's House
14 Beauchamp Tower
15 Devereux Tower
16 Flint Tower
17 Bowyer Tower
18 Brick Tower
19 Martin Tower
20 Constable Tower
21 Broad Arrow Tower
22 Salt Tower
23 Lanthorn Tower
24 Wakefield Tower
25 Bloody Tower
26 Bell Tower
27 Mint Street
28 Casemates

29 Legge's Mount
30 Brass Mount
31 Develin Tower
32 Well Tower
33 Cradle Tower
34 Henry III's Watergate
35 St Thomas's Tower
36 Traitors' Gate
37 Water Lane
38 Byward Tower
39 Middle Tower
40 Lion Tower drawbridge pit (remains)
41 Tower Wharf

Plan of the Tower of London. (*Source, Thomas Römer – Wikimedia Commons*)

Tower also served as a prison – in all but name – to Edward and Richard Plantagenet, whose time (and eventual fate) within the Tower's walls is of course a much more shadowy affair than Anne Boleyn's. However, Edward Plantagenet had a much earlier association with the Tower that began right at the very start of his life, and came about as a result of the Tower serving as the second royal palace in London (after the Palace of Westminster), a role originally established in the thirteenth century and which lasted until the days of Charles II.

The Royal Palace

The Tower of London's sinister reputation as a place of execution and incarceration really dates from Tudor times. During the Middle Ages it was better known as a royal residence, its richly decorated and comfortable rooms dating from the time of Henry III (1216–1272) and his son Edward I (1272–1307). Both they and subsequent monarchs held

The medieval royal palace in the Tower of London occupied this area, now known as the inmost ward, situated between the White Tower and the south wall that abuts the River Thames. The buildings in the background are a former barracks.

court at the Tower, but rarely for very long; Edward I, for instance, spent only fifty-three days here during a reign that lasted thirty-five years. The Palace of Westminster remained the premier royal palace in London, but the Tower was better defended and fortified, and provided a more secure refuge than the Palace of Westminster during times of instability.

The buildings of the medieval palace were situated on the south side of the Tower complex, flanking the southern curtain wall and with direct access through a gateway in this wall from the river. Today only the circular Wakefield Tower and the neighbouring St Thomas's Tower, under which is the infamous river landing stage known as Traitors' Gate, remain as reminders of this palace. To the east of these is the Lanthorn Tower which was also part of the palace, but the current structure was completely rebuilt in the nineteenth century. Most of the other palace buildings – including Edward I's Great Hall – were demolished in the middle of the seventeenth century, the work initiated by Oliver Cromwell and completed two decades later by Charles II. The site of these parts of the palace is now occupied by an extensive patch of greenery flanked to the north by the White Tower and to the east by an undistinguished, red-brick Victorian-era barracks block. (The Tower's main gift shop is built partly under this area of lawn, its subterranean location rendering it pleasingly unobtrusive.) The *Black Book of the Household* from Edward IV's reign describes the palace, in his day, as comprising three separate chambers, with interior decorations that incorporated stained-glass windows inlaid with the royal coat of arms and fleur de lys emblem, and floor tiles decorated with royal leopards and white harts (deer), the emblem of Richard II, who had designed this area. Tapestries and wall paintings probably completed the picture. For today's visitor to the remaining rooms of the medieval palace, the most atmospheric area is the first room in St Thomas's Tower, which has been left bare and unrestored, the grand medieval fireplace still discernable; next door, Edward I's bedchamber has been restored and decorated with replica furniture of his time. The tiny oratory known as the 'chapel over the water' mentioned in records has likewise been restored in a sympathetic though inevitably rather sanitised manner (audio tracks recreate the sound of a crackling fire in the grate). Similarly restored is the Wakefield Tower, a private audience chamber complete nowadays with a luxurious (replica) throne and a high vaulted ceiling that, like the Lanthorn Tower nearby, is a nineteenth-century reconstruction. The latter, however, is enlivened by the displays of some

Above: A re-created interior in the medieval palace of the Tower of London.

Right: The heavily restored Wakefield Tower is part of the former medieval palace in the Tower of London.

extraordinary objects found during restoration work in the Royal Palace, including a fabulous rock crystal chess piece and a rather battered pewter toy knight, the latter a reminder that the Tower has always been home to children (and remains so today), from heirs to the throne to children of servants, military personnel and Tower employees.

It was to the royal palace here that Edward Plantagenet was brought in April 1471 as a babe-in-arms, some five months after his birth at Cheyneygates. As we have seen in Chapter One, by that time Edward's father the king had deposed Henry VI and was ruling his kingdom again from London. But the invasion of Margaret of Anjou, Henry's wife, meant that the political situation was still volatile and young Edward and his mother had to live behind the defensive walls of the Tower rather than make their home in the more vulnerable Palace of Westminster. The following month Edward IV's forces defeated those of Margaret of Anjou at Tewkesbury. Henry VI, at the time a prisoner in the Tower, died shortly afterwards, and indeed was probably murdered by Richard, Duke of Gloucester, though his guilt has ever been proved. But it is possible that baby Edward was in the palatial apartments in the Tower with his mother as Henry was butchered by his uncle in another part of the palace, just a few metres away. The small chapel that adjoins the Wakefield Tower has traditionally been identified as the place of Henry's murder; a plaque set into the floor of the chapel commemorates the event. No wonder that Philippa Gregory has Elizabeth Woodville in *The White Queen* suffer a premonition as she establishes her residence in the Tower with baby Edward. 'It is always a dark building for me, a place of death,' she admits; she had 'always hated the Tower. I know this is why the tall dark place on the edge of the Thames has always filled me with foreboding … I don't want my son to sleep here.'

Of course, Elizabeth's dark premonition came to pass. Edward returned to the palatial apartments in the Tower much later in his life – without his mother, and in very different circumstances. As has already been noted, when the young king was brought to London from Stony Stratford his first place of residence was the Palace of the Bishop of London, located beside St Paul's Cathedral. During this time the Royal Council met both at the Palace and nearby at Richard of Gloucester's London residence, Baynard's Castle. According to the Croyland Chronicle, at one of these meetings 'a discussion took place about removing the king to some place where fewer restrictions would be imposed upon him.' The Duke of Buckingham, Croyland states, suggested the Tower, as tradition had it that this was where monarchs resided prior to their coronation (which was set for 22 June). Edward was duly moved there some time between 9 and 16 May. It was a shrewd move on Richard's part, as Edward was visibly being treated as a monarch should be – yet residing in the Tower meant that he was distanced both from his mother (who was in sanctuary at Westminster) and from the political machinations over the succession that were unfolding in Baynard's Castle and in the Palace of Westminster. In *Richard III* Shakespeare gives these events a different narrative context, having Richard (not Buckingham) suggest that Edward repose in the Tower shortly after their arrival in the capital from Stony Stratford: 'If I may counsel you, some day or two,' Richard advises, 'Your highness shall repose you at the Tower'. The boy naively responds that he knows that the Tower had been built by Julius Caesar (a popular tradition at the time, when the White Tower was known as 'Caesar's Tower') and Richard flatters him in that assumption, cynically observing in an aside that 'So wise so young, they say, do never / live long.'

From 9 May, Edward issued grants, warrants and other proclamations in his own name from the Tower of London – 'by the advice of our dearest uncle, the Duke of Gloucester, Protector and Defensor of this our Realm, during our young age, and by the advice of the lords of Our Council'. The initials 'RE' (Rex Edwardus) at the bottom of these documents tends to be rather sketchy as Edward learned the business of kingship. During this time Edward gathered around himself a small court, at the heart of which was Lord Hastings, a key adviser and friend of his father who came from a family of Yorkshire gentry fiercely loyal to the House of York. Hastings was, according to the chronicler Dominic Mancini, the 'accomplice and partner of the King's privy pleasures' – the pleasures concerned largely consisting of eating, drinking and whoring. As Richard consolidated his own power – on 10 May he took control of the navy from Sir Edward Woodville, the queen's brother – Edward's court began to look more and more like an unofficial opposition to his authority. Official meetings of the Royal Council took place in the Tower though there is no record that Edward attended any of them. And it is clear that Edward was merely rubber stamping the Council's proclamations; as the Croyland Chronicle has it, Gloucester had 'power to order and forbid in every matter, just like any other king'. And then on 13 June Richard presided over a council meeting that had an extraordinarily bloody end – and one which directly affected the life of Edward Plantagenet.

The meeting took place within the thick walls of the White Tower, across the courtyard from Edward's quarters in the Royal Palace. Mancini relates that shortly before nine o'clock the Councillors were seated and were waiting 'to salute the Protector, as was their custom'. They believed they had been summoned to discuss Edward's coronation. According to Thomas More, Richard's mood at the opening of the meeting was jovial. His first act was to order John Morton, the Bishop of Ely, to have some strawberries sent up from his London residence which was situated around a mile away in Holborn (the palace was demolished in the eighteenth century but its location is remembered today in the name of Ely Place, which leads off Charterhouse Street). Richard then left, to return after an hour and a half in a very different state of mind. More accuses him of making an extraordinary outburst in front of the assembled councillors: 'What do men deserve,' Richard asked, in a state of fury, 'for having plotted the destruction of me, being so near of blood to the king, and protector of his royal person and realm?' More has Hastings respond that 'certainly, if they have done so heinously, they are worthy of a heinous punishment,' to which Richard responded 'I tell thee they have done it, and that I will make good upon thy body, traitor!' He then accused the councillors of having prepared an ambush for him. Armed men appeared – either from the next-door room or from behind a curtain, sources differ – and a violent scuffle ensued, which resulted in shed blood and open wounds. Hastings was dragged away and was told to see a priest, 'for, by St Paul,' Richard snarled, 'I will not to dinner until I see thy head off' (dinner traditionally took place at eleven o'clock, so Hastings knew he faced imminent death). More says that Hastings was dragged to the area of green outside the Tower's principal chapel, which lies to the northwest of the White Tower. (The current building, the Chapel of St Peter ad Vincula, or St Peter in Chains, dates from 1520; the building that occupied this site previously was a Norman foundation.) Those buried within this airy and beautiful building include Anne Boleyn, Catherine Howard, Lady Jane Grey and Thomas Cromwell. All were executed, like Hastings, in the area to its immediate south, known as Tower Green (public beheadings took place in a different location, outside the walls of the Tower on Tower Hill):

'and there, on a squared piece of timber [an executioner] strake off his head' wrote Thomas More – who was to die in the exact same place and manner over half a century after Hastings, and who was also buried in St Peter's Chapel (Hastings was given the honour of a burial at St George's Chapel, Windsor). There seems to have been no form of judicial process in Hastings' execution (though some historians support the contention that Hastings was actually executed a week after the fateful council meeting, in which case there would probably have been a trial). There is also a dispute as to whether Edward could have seen the execution from his rooms in the Royal Palace, and if so whether ensuring that he had a view of it was an act of spite on Richard's part. Certainly the west windows of the royal palace looked directly towards Tower Green, and the commotion surrounding the execution would have commanded attention.

Whatever the exact circumstances surrounding Hastings' death, it seems that Richard, to whom Hastings had once been a faithful confidant, made the decision to have him executed as he had become too close to Edward. Mancini maintains that 'after Hastings was removed, all the attendants who had waited upon the king were debarred access to him.' It is certainly the case that Edward was politically isolated following the execution of Hastings; today, however, Lord Hastings is known in the mythology of the Tower not as the supporter of Edward Plantagenet, but as the first person to be executed on Tower Green. Another six beheadings took place here over the next century or so, and in 1743 three soldiers, all members of Scotland's Black Watch regiment, were shot by firing squad at this spot, bringing the total number of executions here to ten. Today all ten are commemorated by a contemporary, circular monument designed by the sculptor Brian Catling, which has a crystal cushion at its heart, and an inscription around its base that reads 'gentle visitor pause a while: where you stand, death cut away the light of many days ... may they rest in peace while we walk the generations around their strife and courage, under these restless skies.'

With Hastings out of the picture, Richard – according to Mancini – 'therefore resolved to get into his power the Duke of York ... for [he] foresaw that the Duke of York would by legal right succeed to the throne if his brother was arrested.' Richard's intentions were submitted to his councillors at a meeting on Monday 16 June, where he submitted to council – again, according to Mancini – how improper it was that the

This memorial sculpture commemorates all those executed on Tower Green, including Lord Hastings, whose execution was ordered by Richard of Gloucester after he was seen to be too close politically to Edward Plantagenet.

king should be 'crowned in the absence of his brother, who, on account of his nearness of kin and his station, ought to play an important part in the ceremony'. The younger prince was being held against his will in the Westminster sanctuary, Richard argued, which was a place of refuge, not detention. He also felt that young Edward, isolated in the royal palace, had need of a playmate. Later on that same day Richard personally visited the Westminster sanctuary along with Buckingham and Archbishop Bourchier – as we have already seen in Chapter One – and brought Richard of Shrewsbury to the Tower, where he was installed in the royal palace with his brother. 'It was true that Edward was lonely,' Vanora Bennett writes of their meeting in her novel *Portrait of an Unknown Woman*. 'His face lit up at the sight of his brother walking into the big, echoing apartment. He looked six inches taller than at Christmas, and much thinner ... all Edward said, through his huge smile, was "knucklebones"' – an ancient game popular in the Middle Ages that involved the dice-like throwing of small animal bones.

The Bloody Tower

The boys might not have been together long in the royal palace; a few days, if that. Mancini maintains that soon after Richard's arrival,

> all the attendants who had waited upon the king were debarred from him. He and his brother were withdrawn into the inner apartments of the Tower proper, and day by day began to be seen more rarely behind the bars and windows, till at length they ceased to appear altogether.

Tradition maintains that the place the boys were moved to was the Garden Tower, a two-storey stone building that overlooks the Tower's central courtyard on one side, and the alley known as Water Lane on the other. Part of Henry III's additions to the Tower's defences, the Garden Tower was equipped with

The Garden Tower – or Bloody Tower – is the traditional location of the princes' imprisonment.

Above: The Garden Tower - or Bloody Tower - is the traditional location of the princes' imprisonment.

Left: The Bloody Tower is the traditional location of the princes' imprinoment. Displays in the Tower's upper room now tell their story.

126

The famous painting by the French artist Paul Delaroche depicting Edward and Richard Plantagenet imprisoned in the Tower.

a massive portcullis (the grooves for its lowering and raising can still be seen) and controlled access to the Tower of London's inner courtyard. Today it's through the Garden Tower's central archway that most visitors enter the Tower of London when they first arrive. However, visitors know this tower better as the 'Bloody Tower', a sinister moniker that dates from the suicide here in the 1580s of Henry Percy, the eighth Earl of Northumberland. Others who suffered imprisonment here included Archbishop Cranmer, and Bishops Ridley and Latimer, who were condemned to death for heresy, and were burned at the stake at Oxford in 1556; 'Hanging' Judge Jeffreys who had sentenced over 300 people to be executed or transported to the Penal colonies at the 'Bloody Assizes'; and Sir Walter Raleigh, who wrote his unfinished *History of the World* here, and who conducted scientific experiments in the garden. The Tower adjoins the Wakefield Tower and lies across Water Lane from St Thomas's Tower (and the infamous Traitors' Gate), both of which are parts of the medieval royal palace that still stand; so in some ways, rather than being moved from the royal palace, it could be said, the boys were simply confined to a more secure part of it. Yet it is important to remember that no sources confirm that it was here that the boys were kept; it seems that the Bloody Tower's reputation as a place of murder and incarceration led to it being identified as the traditional place of their imprisonment and death – a response, in part, to a need to identify a sense of 'history where it happened'. The fact that the gardens of the Lieutenant's house adjoin the Bloody Tower (and gave it its original name) – and that contemporary reports suggest that the princes were often seen playing 'in the gardens' – give further credence to this being where they were kept, though some historians have suggested the larger Lanthorn Tower, also part of the medieval royal palace and built specifically as the lodgings for Henry III's queen (and later used as residential quarters by Henry VII), might have been a more likely location.

Even as the princes were moved from the royal palace into the Lanthorn or Garden Tower, preparations for Edward Plantagenet's coronation were gathering pace. The accounts of Piers Curteys, Keeper of the Royal Wardrobe, show Edward's coronation robes were ready for him to wear at the grand occasion in Westminster Abbey. They comprised a short gown of crimson cloth-of-gold lined with green damask, blue velvet and purple velvet, a doublet of black satin and a bonnet of purple velvet. But some time between 17 and 21 June, Richard postponed the Coronation indefinitely (though the Tudor chronicler Richard Grafton maintains that a new date was set, of 2 November). On the 22 – the date on which the coronation was originally scheduled – the Dean of St Paul's Cathedral, Dr Ralph Shaa (or Shaw), the half-brother of London's Lord Mayor, preached a sermon at St Paul's Cross, an open-air pulpit in the grounds of the cathedral from which many important religious and political statements were made. In his sermon Dr Shaa announced that Edward and Richard Plantagenet were illegitimate on the grounds that their father, King Edward IV, had already entered a pre-contract of marriage when he married their mother, Elizabeth Woodville. According to Shaa (and of course Richard), the pre-contract had been arranged with a Lady Eleanor Butler, the daughter of John Talbot, Earl of Shrewsbury. The Croyland Chronicle picks up the story:

> It was set forth ... that the sons of King Edward were bastards, on the ground that he had contracted a marriage with one Lady Eleanor Butler before his marriage to Queen

> Elizabeth … so that, at the present time, no certain and
> uncorrupted lineal blood could be found of Richard, Duke of
> York, except in the person of Richard, Duke of Gloucester.

Edward's 'marriage' to Lady Eleanor had been celebrated clandestinely;
there had been no formal church wedding, and no reading of banns. The
Bishop of Bath and Wells, Robert Stillington, had actually performed the
ceremony and disclosed this claim to the Royal Council; but with both
Edward and Lady Eleanor dead it was of course impossible to prove his
story, as only Edward, Eleanor and Stillington were present. Stillington
maintained that in the eyes of the church Edward's later marriage was
invalid. Yet a swirl of arguments surrounds this supposed marriage and
its consequence: would a bishop actually have performed such a marriage?
Edward and Richard Plantagenet were born after Eleanor's death – so did
this actually render them legitimate? And if the second spouse was not
aware of the first, then did this make the offspring of this second marriage
bastards? Furthermore, in matters pertaining to the throne, was it secular
law decided by parliament, or canon law decided by clerics, that held sway?
It wasn't even clear that bastards were unable to succeed to the throne;
William the Conqueror was illegitimate, as were Queens Elizabeth and
Mary (the princes' great nieces) in the following century. Nonetheless, on
25 June the Duke of Buckingham repeated the claims to the assembled
members of the Lords and Commons, and the following day selected Lords
gathered at Baynard's Castle to proclaim Richard king. Barely two weeks
later, on 6 July, he was crowned King of England in Westminster Abbey.

What then became of the princes is, of course, one of the great mysteries
of English history. Dominic Mancini left England for Italy in the middle
of July and reported that by then the princes had,

> ceased to appear altogether … I have seen many men burst
> forth into tears and lamentations when mention was made
> of Edward V after his removal from men's sight; and already
> there was a suspicion that he had been done away with.
> Whether, however, he has been done away with, and by what
> manner of death, so far I have not at all discovered.

(The key phrase in the above passage – 'done away with' – is controversial.
Mancini wrote in Latin and some modern writers have said that his term

'sublatum' should be translated as 'removed' or 'carried off' rather than 'done away with', rendering the meaning of his phrase 'what manner of death has carried him off' – which suggests that Edward's death could have been natural.) The Great Chronicle of London maintains that 'the children of King Edward were seen ... playing in the garden of the Tower on sundry times,' though it is unclear whether this referred to the period before or after Richard's coronation. Thomas More claimed that both boys were,

> shut up, and all others removed from them, only one called Black Will or Will Slaughter except, set to serve them and see them sure. After which time the Prince never tied his points [of his hose] nor aught wrought of himself, but with that young babe his brother lingered in thought and heaviness and wretchedness.

Will Slaughter was the boys' gaoler and servant; others around the princes at this time included Dr John Argentine, who was later physician to Henry VII's son Prince Arthur and the Provost of King's College Cambridge, who was probably the person with the greatest access to them. Mancini later reported 'that the king, like a victim prepared for sacrifice, sought remission of his sins by daily confession and penance, because he believed death was facing him.' Edward must have known that a number of his predecessors – Edward II, Richard II and Henry VI – had all been murdered by their supplanters; maybe Molinet was also thinking of this when he wrote that Edward 'was very melancholic, recognising the malice of his uncle', fearing the same fate would befall him. The Croyland Chronicle maintains that the princes remained 'in the Tower in the custody of certain persons appointed for that purpose', and reckons this continued into September – the last mention of their whereabouts. One of those 'certain persons' was Sir Robert Brackenbury, one of Richard's most loyal henchmen, who was appointed constable of the Tower by him on July 17.

Thomas More's account of what happened next is compelling in terms of drama – though has been scorned by many commentators as regards its veracity. More says that when King Richard's 'royal progress' of the summer of 1483 – that is, his tours of major cities of the realm – reached Gloucester he,

> devised as he rode to fulfill that thing which he before had intended. For his mind gave him that, his nephews living, men would not reckon that he could have right to the realm;

he thought, therefore, without delay to rid them, as though the killing of his kinsmen could amend his cause and make him a kindly king.

Richard then sent a retainer named John Green to Brackenbury with a letter requesting that Brackenbury should kill the boys; but Brackenbury refused, and so Richard approached another of his retainers, Sir James Tyrrell, and asked him to take a slightly different letter to Brackenbury, this one demanding that the constable hand over to Tyrrell 'all the keys of the Tower for one night, to the end he might there accomplish the king's pleasure.' Tyrrell has an interesting and complex background; his father, Sir John Tyrrell, had been executed in 1462 for attempting to murder King Edward IV, but Sir James fared better, fighting for Edward at the Battle of Tewkesbury and being knighted afterwards. More asserted that Tyrrell devised a plan that the princes 'should be murdered in their beds', and put this into action on 15 August, appointing his housekeeper John Dighton, and a common criminal named Miles Forest (a man who, according to More, was 'fleshed in murder before his time'), to do the deed. The two men,

> came into the chamber and suddenly lapped [the two boys] up among the clothes, so bewrapped them and entangled them, keeping down by force the feather bed and pillows hard into their mouths, that within a while [they were] smothered and stifled; their breath failing, they gave up to God their innocent souls into the joys of heaven, leaving to the tormentors their bodies dead in the bed.

Afterwards the two men lay the bodies 'naked upon the bed and fetched Sir James to see them.' The chronicler Polydore Vergil also adheres to these versions of events, suggesting (like More) that Brackenbury was unwilling to implement the original 'cruel' and 'horrible' order to murder the princes, forcing Richard to,

> anon [commit] the charge of hastening that slaughter unto another, that is to say James Tyrrell, who, being forced to do the kings commandment, rode sorrowfully to London, and, to the worst example that hath been almost ever heard of, murdered those babes of the royal issue.

131

Vergil's story was later corroborated by the author and printer (and friend of Thomas More) John Rastell, who in his 1529 chronicle *The Past Time of the People* lent a grisly twist to this scenario. In this version of events, young Richard at first escapes from the murders and hides under the bed,

> and there lay naked awhile till they had smothered the young king so that he was surely dead. And after that one of them took [Richard] from under the bedstead and held his face down to the ground with one hand, and with his other hand cut his throat with his dagger.

Shakespeare follows Thomas More's version of events in his play *Richard III*. But the murder is not dramatised. Instead, we see (in Act IV Scene 1) Elizabeth Woodville outside the Tower of London, trying to gain access to her sons and being refused entry by Brackenbury, whereupon she laments 'Pity, you ancient stones, those tender babes / Whom envy hath immured within your walls! / Rough cradle for such little pretty ones!' (In Richard Loncraine's 1995 film *Richard III*, the old Bankside power station on the Thames, now the Tate Modern, stands in for the Tower of London, and the scene is filmed outside its blank, forbidding walls.) In the following scene, Richard asks Buckingham to kill the boys: 'Shall I be plain?' he demands. 'I wish the bastards dead / And I would have it suddenly perform'd' – but Buckingham hesitates, so Richard instead speaks with Tyrrell of 'the two deep enemies / Foes to my rest and my sweet sleep's disturbers ... I mean those bastards in the Tower.' Tyrrell, a man always portrayed as being seeped in oily ambition and a desire for advancement, assures Richard that 'soon I'll rid you of the fear from them'. When the next scene opens the boys are dead. In a soliloquy Tyrrell declaims that 'The tyrannous and bloody deed is done,' calling it 'The most arch of piteous massacre / That ever yet this land was guilty of'. He goes on to state that Dighton had reported to him that he and Forest had 'smothered / The most replenished sweet work of nature' as instructed.

By contrast, the novelist Reay Tannahill provides a full dramatisation of the murder in *The Seventh Son* – using More's narrative as her guide. She recounts how the murderers crept 'noiselessly along the roofs of the royal apartments' of the Tower on a 'cool night following a hot and sticky day', when a faint mist 'was wafting from the Thames into the precincts of the Tower of London…. They had been instructed to leave no signs of violence, so that the deaths would be a mystery – which ruled out the knives they would have used from choice, and left them with only one option.' Once inside the princes' room the murderers took a mattress and,

> taking one end each, dropped it over the boys' heads and leaned on it, feeling through the stuffing for the noses and mouths that were to be stopped for ever … the children fought, chokingly, against it, their arms waving, hands clawing, and legs kicking out wildly. The two men continued to hold the mattress down for what seemed like an eternity after all movement ceased. Then they took it away and gave a hiccup of fright to see the dead eyes staring at them.

Forest and Dighton then scarpered, leaving the bodies where they were and taking a few trinkets from the boys' rooms with them as souvenirs.

Whether or not he organised the murders in the Bloody Tower on that August night, Tyrrell certain secured his advancement. Richard appointed him High Sheriff of Cornwall, and later the Governor of Guisnes in the Pale of Calais. But in 1501 Tyrrell lent his support to Edmund de la Pole, by then the leading Yorkist contender for throne, in a conspiracy against Henry VII. Tyrrell allegedly confessed to the murder of the princes during his interrogation following his arrest at Calais. However the confession no longer exists and evidence that Tyrrell actually made it is scant. Many have suggested that Tyrrell was simply used as a scapegoat by a Tudor regime anxious to blacken the name of Richard III, and that his confession would deter future pretenders to the throne of the likes of Perkin Warbeck and Lambert Simnel, both of whom had claimed to be the grown-up Richard of Shrewsbury. Where Thomas More obtained his information regarding the role of Tyrrell, Forest and Dighton, and the exact way in which the princes were murdered is unknown; many have claimed that much of it was simply culled from rumours circulating at the time.

As for the Bloody Tower, it's unfortunately been restored and sanitised to such a degree that any sense of history that might have lingered there has long gone. Downstairs there's a mock-up of Sir Walter Raleigh's desk, complete with papers, reference books and quill, while upstairs, all contemporary beams and whitewashed walls are given over to display panels about the princes and their supposed murder in this room, which is just large enough not to be described as 'poky'. On one wall a contemporary film entitled *Crown of Blood* is projected. This is an animated take on the princes' story by the illustrator, animator and designer Paul Duffield which was commissioned by Historic Royal Palaces in 2005 for the Tower of London. It's filmed entirely in black, white and red (for the blood) in the crudely brutal style of modern manga comics, and is laden with ominously swirling clouds, ominously circling ravens, ominously slamming doors and ominously echoing laughter from the princes as they hurtle along passageways, fall down nightmarish shafts, crown each other with laurel wreaths and otherwise await their inevitable fate (the film shows them, inaccurately, arriving at the Tower together in an open carriage, waving to the crowds; it's not hard to track down on YouTube). By contrast, *Crown of Blood* is accompanied by a scene from Laurence Olivier's classic (very colourful, though rather stagey) 1955 film of *Richard III*; King Richard demonstrates to Tyrrell (using, ridiculously, a crimson cushion) how the princes are to be killed, which is followed by a cutaway to the murder scene, where Dighton and Forest are about to commit the deed while the boys lie together in bed (cue some dramatic chords). As to other cinematic representations of the supposed events that took place in the Bloody Tower, Richard Loncraine's 1995 film gives a similarly brief though much more shocking rendition of this scene – a red cloth is forced over the blond, sleeping head of Richard of Shrewsbury – while the 1939 film *Tower of London* shows young Richard making sure his pet hawk is asleep before getting into bed beside his brother, a precursor to the inevitable shove on the door (from Mord, Richard III's entirely fictional club-footed executioner, played by the legendary horror actor Boris Karloff) and deathly screams as the princes are smothered; Roger Corman's later film of the same title follows the lead set by Shakespeare, and does not depict the deaths of the princes.

The stairs in the White Tower and the Discovery of the Skeletons

The White Tower is the oldest, most monumental and most iconic part of the Tower of London. It was built as a fortress and as a place for ceremonial functions; in 1240 Henry III had the building covered in whitewash, and during the time of the princes' stay (many would say imprisonment) in the Tower of London the building looked largely as it does now, although other buildings (demolished in the 1880s) adjoined it, and the elegant turret roofs were not added until the 1530s. Inside, however, the function of the White Tower had changed since the time of its construction, and much of its two vast floors had been largely converted into storehouses for weapons and ammunition. Today this role lives on in the White Tower's extensive displays of armour and weaponry.

For reasons of security the White Tower has no ground floor access. The main entrance doorway is 'suspended' a good few metres up the south flank of the Tower. Today this is the main doorway for visitors, and is accessed by an external flight of wooden steps with two landings. (In former times, access to this doorway would have been gained by enclosed spiral stone staircases topped by turrets – all long since demolished.) Two thirds of the way up the wooden staircase – and often ignored by visitors anxious to see Henry VIII's armour and other treasures of the Royal Armouries collection – the second landing gives a view into an alcove that houses part of an ancient staircase that appears to lead to and from nowhere, having long been walled off. The staircase once gave direct access to the Chapel of St John the Evangelist, a beautiful Norman foundation that was incorporated into the White Tower's second floor during its original construction (the top of the walled-off staircase can still be seen just outside the chapel's entrance). Beside the staircase is a plaque that reads, in block capitals: 'The tradition of the Tower has always pointed out this as the stair under which the bones of Edward the 5th and his brother were found in Charles the 2nd's time and from whence they were removed to Westminster Abbey'. Sir Christopher Wren, who was commissioned to construct the tomb that housed the bones in Westminster Abbey, stated in *Parentalia* (his posthumously published writings) that the bones were discovered 'about ten feet deep in the ground as the workmen were taking away the stairs which led from the royal lodgings into the chapel of the White Tower'. This seems to suggest that the identified staircase is the right one – no other staircase led from the royal palace to the chapel – though Wren was not an eyewitness to the discovery of the bones, which is perhaps why the identification of this particular staircase as the correct location remains a 'tradition'.

The version of the fate of the Princes that has them killed and buried at the Tower is full of stories of staircases. Thomas More's account of the

The entrance to the White Tower, the oldest part of the Tower of London, is today reached by a wooden staircase. The alcove half way up marks the position of the interior stone staircase under which the princes were supposedly buried.

murder of the princes states that Sir James Tyrrell had the bodies buried 'at the foot of some stairs, mightily deep in the ground, under a great heap of stones', but added that 'a priest of Sir Robert Brackenbury later took up the bodies and secretly interred them in such a place … which only

Above left: The stairs leading to the White Tower. In the centre of the photograph is the alcove with the memorial plaque to the princes.

Above right: The stone staircase within the White Tower under which the princes were supposedly buried led up to this Norman chapel dedicated to St John the Evangelist.

he knew, and has never since come to light…', so that in the end, 'their bodies were cast God knows where'. But More was unclear as to the exact location of this staircase, and reports of the unearthing of the skeletons in the 1670s also seem to be vague about precisely which staircase was being repaired when the remains were found – heaping yet more conjecture onto the already fraught controversy surrounding the bones that were later interred in Westminster Abbey (as described in in Chapter One).

The discovery of what was assumed to be the princes' remains came in 1674, during a time when Charles II had ordered extensive repairs and renovations to the Tower. Already much of the former medieval palace had been demolished; the workmen then knocked down the crumbling turret and spiral staircase that led up to the White Tower's main entrance, before setting to work on the staircase that led directly to St John's Chapel. It was 10ft beneath the foundations of this crumbling staircase that a large wooden chest was uncovered, which was discovered to contain the skeletons of two children. The taller child lay on its back; the other had been placed on top, face down. One eyewitness to the discovery was

This memorial plaque in the White Tower commemorates the discovery of the bodies that were assumed to be those of the princes and which were subsequently buried in Westminster Abbey.

John Knight, principal surgeon to Charles II, who reported that 'about ten foot in the ground were found the bones of two striplings in (as it seem'd) a wooden chest, which upon the survey were found proportionable to the ages of the two brothers, viz about thirteen and eleven years. The skull of one being entire, the other broken.' However his report was quoted in a study from 1707 – some forty years later – and the original source has been lost. Another contemporary report attributed to an anonymous eye-witness gives an account of the event:

> This day I, standing by the opening, saw workmen dig out of a stairway in the White Tower the bones of those two Princes who were foully murdered by Richard III. They were small bones of lads in their teens, and there were pieces of rag and velvet about them … being fully recognised to be the bones of those two princes, they were carefully put aside in a stone coffin or coffer.

138

Velvet gains its smoothness from being woven using a special loom; in the Middle Ages it was an expensive luxury item (manufactured in Italy and the Low Countries) and so the conclusion was reached that the buried children must have been high-born. Yet when the contents of the princes' supposed burial urn in Westminster Abbey were examined in 1933 there was no velvet present (it would have survived, as had the linen shroud of Richard of Shrewsbury's 'wife', Anne Mowbray). So this really gets us no nearer to concluding whether or not these were the bones of the princes.

The Tower of London has, throughout its history, been a home to children. This continues to this day; many staff members (including beefeaters) live in accommodation within the precincts of the Tower, with their families. Given this, it is not surprising that the Tower has yielded other bodies of children over time. One of the most famous of these discoveries was made during the time of the incarceration of Sir Walter Raleigh, who was imprisoned in the Bloody Tower 120 years after the disappearance of the princes. An account of this gruesome discovery appears on the flyleaf of a 1641 edition of Thomas More's biography of Richard III, owned by a man named Webb. The account maintains that in around 1615 a blocked-off passageway in the king's lodgings in the Royal Apartments was broken through, and the bones of two young children aged around 6 and 8 were then discovered laid out on a table. The 'Jo. Webb' who signed this account can be identified as John Webb, who was deputy to Inigo Jones, Surveyor of the King's Works from 1615 to 1643, and who, as a trained architect, would have had a good knowledge of the layout of the Tower. Webb wrote that,

> the wall of the passage to the King's Lodgings then sounding hollow, was taken down and at the place marked A [on his accompanying sketch] was found a little room about 7 or 8 ft square, wherein there stood a table and upon it the bones of two children supposed of 6 or 8 yeares of age, which by the aforesaid nobles and all present were credibly believed to be the carcasses of Edward the 5th and his brother the then Duke of York.

Webb cited a Mr Johnson, son of Sir Robert Johnson, and also names a Mr Palmer and a Mr Henry Cogan, officers of the mint, as eyewitnesses.

No account is given as to what became of these bones. A remarkably similar account of this discovery was later published in 1680 by the French historian Louis Aubery du Maurier, who reported that,

> in Queen Elizabeth's time, the Tower of London being full of prisoners of State, on account of the frequent conspiracies against her person, as they were troubled to find room for them all, they bethought themselves of opening a door of a chamber that had been walled up for a long time; and they found in this chamber upon a bed two little carcasses with two halters around their necks. These were the skeletons of King Edward V and the Duke of York, his brother, whom their uncle Richard the cruel had strangled to get the Crown. But the prudent Princess, not willing to revive the memory of such an execrable deed, had the door walled up as before.

The discrepancy in these sources – one attributing the find to the reign of James I, the second to the reign of his predecessor Elizabeth – has been much debated by historians, as has the fact that the children whose skeletons these were died at a much younger age than the princes.

Other accounts of discoveries of child skeletons in the Tower abound. Many skeletons were unearthed when the moat was drained in the 1830s, while the discovery in 1977 of the skeleton of a male aged 13–16 during an archeological excavation of the inmost ward of the tower caused huge excitement when it was posited that this might be the body of Edward V – only for this to be dashed when the skeleton was firmly dated to the Iron Age. That the Tower is chock-full of bones from various eras beneath its various floors makes ascribing any one set of bones to a particular person fraught with supposition. Is it conceivable that the bodies discovered in 1674 could have been centuries old, even from the Roman or pre-Norman era? (Velvet was only introduced to Europe in the Middle Ages, so if we accept the account of it being found with the bones then this avenue of enquiry can be quashed.) Other finds have turned out to be bones of apes that had escaped from the Tower menagerie – which may account for the fact that the urn in Westminster Abbey contains a number of animal bones. And so the conjecture and supposition continues – all of it a result of the fact that really no one knows what became of the princes following Richard's coronation on 6 July 1483.

Chapter Five

The Aftermath – Ghosts and Tombs, Impostors and Battlefields

For many, the trail of the princes runs out at the Tower of London – either in the Bloody Tower, where the princes might have been murdered, or in the bricked-up staircase in the White Tower, where their bodies might have been buried. Thus freed of bodily encumbrances, the souls of the dead princes were then free to haunt their murderer, King Richard III, as, some two years after their incarceration in the Tower, he prepared to do battle at Bosworth Field against Henry Tudor, the Lancastrian pretender to the throne of England. The Croyland Chronicle describes the visitations that apparently tormented the king on the eve of the battle, which was fought 3 miles south of the small town of Market Bosworth, in the heart of England, on 22 August 1485. 'The king ... had seen that night a multitude of demons apparently surrounding him,' the chronicle recounts; these apparitions turned the king's countenance 'pale and deathly' as a result. Shakespeare played on this theme in his play *Richard III*, relating (in Act V, Scene III) how Richard is haunted by the ghosts of those he has murdered on his way to the throne, each victim tormenting him with the prophetic admonishment that he should 'despair and die'. After the ghosts of King Henry VI, Henry's son Edward, and Richard's own brother the Duke of Clarence have made an appearance, a further succession of ghosts shimmer into view, all of whom have played a part in the princes' story – Earl Rivers (Edward Plantagenet's guardian), Sir Richard Grey (the princes' half-brother, who was arrested at Stony Stratford), Edward's chamberlain Thomas Vaughan (also arrested at Stony Stratford) and Lord Hastings (Edward's key supporter as Richard took control of the royal council and moved the princes to the Tower of London). Then, finally, it is the turn of the princes themselves to appear in front of Richard. 'Dream on thy cousins smother'd in the Tower,' the two boys tell him in unison. 'Let us be led within thy bosom, Richard / And weigh thee down to ruin, shame, and death! / Thy nephews' souls bid thee despair and die!' They then turn and make a direct address to Henry Tudor, known in the play as the Earl of Richmond: 'Sleep, Richmond, sleep in peace, and wake in joy,' they plead. 'Good angels guard thee from the boar's [ie Richard's] annoy! / Live, and beget a happy race of kings! Edward's unhappy sons do bid thee flourish.'

Yet many authorities – and legends – contend that the princes, or at least one of them, still lived, in the Tower of London or elsewhere, even as Richard III fell at Bosworth and was buried afterwards in a priory at Leicester, some 9 miles to the east of the battle site. If the boys were still languishing in the Tower after Bosworth they might, of course, have been murdered by Henry Tudor, as they had a much more valid claim to the throne than he did And of course Henry had to overturn Richard III's proclamation that the princes were illegitimate, as he did not want his new wife, their sister Elizabeth, to be afflicted with this same stain. Alternatively, Henry – or Richard before him – might have ordered that the boys be released, to be given new identities and to forge new lives for themselves away from London. Many theories – from those soberly accepted by historians as having more than a grain of possibility about them, to those which are just plain wacky – have been put forward as to what became of one or both boys, if they had survived the Tower. These theories are given some credence by a number of chroniclers, including Polydore Vergil, who revised the manuscript of *Anglia Historia* before its publication in Basel in 1534 and mentioned in the new edition a rumour that the boys 'had migrated secretly to some other country'. But if one or both of them was still alive, where were they living? Audrey Williamson, whose 1981 book *The Mystery of the Princes* keeps an open mind on their fate, investigated the tradition of the family of the princes' supposed murderer, James Tyrrell, which purports that during the reign of Henry VII the boys were living with their mother at Gipping Hall near Stowmarket in Suffolk, the Tyrrell family's ancestral home that was demolished in the 1850s. A fanciful legend – and one with no evidence to support it. Another theory along the same lines, propagated particularly by the revisionist historians Sir Clements Markham and Jeremy Potter, maintains that once released from the Tower, the boys were sent to live in Sheriff Hutton Castle in Yorkshire, one of Richard's northern strongholds, in a household that included a number of Yorkist children – among them

Richard's bastard sons, and the 10-year-old Edward Plantagenet, the 17th Earl of Warwick, who as the son of the executed George, Duke of Clarence, had a major claim on the throne of England. Evidence for this is limited to accounts of clothing being delivered to 'The Lord Bastard' at Sheriff Hutton and a comment by Polydore Vergil to the effects that a boy of 15 was moved from this castle in 1485 on the orders of Henry VII; although this fits in with the age of Edward Plantagenet, the older prince, it is likely that Vergil was referring to Edward, Earl of Warwick, and was simply incorrect about his age.

Another possibility, of course, is that one or both boys died of natural causes soon after their imprisonment. It has been suggested that Edward's treatment at the hands of Dr Argentine came as a result of him being afflicted by the bone infection osteomyelitis, which in the Middle Ages was fatal. Thomas More records that Elizabeth Woodville told Archbishop Bourchier, when she was in sanctuary in 1483, that her oldest son was 'sore diseased with sickness'; and though no other writers have observed this, it is a credible assumption that Edward might indeed have died of this or another disease during the time he was confined in the Tower.

Sheriff Hutton Castle, one of Richard III's strongholds in Yorkshire. Some say that the princes were spirited away from the Tower of London and were sent here to assume new identities. (*Source, Shaun Conway - Wikimedia Commons*)

But for both princes to die of natural causes would have been fortuitous (for their enemies) and coincidental – and it is unlikely that Richard III would have covered up their deaths; instead they would have been given burials commensurate with their status as heirs to a king of England. That Edward died, and Richard survived, to be given another identity later on in his life, seems more plausible – and indeed is a theory that has seeped into popular culture; the first series of the classic BBC comedy *Blackadder* presents Richard III (played by the comedian Peter Cook) as 'a kind and thoughtful man' who cherishes his nephews instead of murdering them; Richard of Shrewsbury then grows up into 'a big strong boy' in the form of booming-voiced Brian Blessed, and assumes the crown as Richard IV, only to be later written out of history by the victorious Henry Tudor after the Battle of Bosworth (Rowan Atkinson's character Edmund Plantagenet is the grown-up Richard's son). Fanciful of course, but it is this version of events – that Richard of Shrewsbury survived to adulthood to assume a new identity – that informs the stories of the four figures that the rest of this chapter is concerned with, namely Lambert Simnel and Perkin Warbeck, the 'pretenders' to the throne of England during the reign of Henry VII; the noted Tudor physician John Clement; and a labourer from Kent named Richard of Eastwell. Following their trail takes us to two rather unlikely places – namely the Belgian city of Mechelen and the tiny hamlet of Eastwell, near Ashford in Kent.

To Mechelen, and the Tomb of John Clement

Mechelen, located midway between Antwerp and Brussels, is a handsome Flemish-speaking city that is often overlooked on the Low Countries tourist trail. It is the home of the Primate of Belgium and is the country's ecclesiastical capital; besides a stupendous Gothic cathedral the city presents its best face in the form of a charming main square and an absorbing waterfront, where – in the way of these things – former warehouses and industrial premises have been transformed into a panoply of restaurants, bars and galleries whose terraces open out onto the River Dijle. The *Rough Guide to Belgium* describes the place as a 'pleasant and appealing town' whose 'provincial atmosphere' comes as something of a surprise, particularly as most visitors come to Mechelen on day trips from the busy cosmopolitan hubs of Antwerp (Belgium's second largest city) or Brussels itself (Mechelen is around twenty minutes on the train from both). If Mechelen seems a little bypassed now, this was certainly not the case in the Middle Ages, when this was one of the great cities of medieval Flanders, attracting a creative community of printers, painters, and composers, the latter working in the polyphonic tradition that reached its zenith in late medieval and Renaissance times. Although the prominent scars of more recent history loom large in the city – there's an informative museum detailing Mechelen's role as a transit camp for Belgium's Jews, who were gathered here before being sent 'east' to the Nazi death camps in Poland – it's impossible to ignore the legacy of the Middle Ages, when for a time Charles the Bold, Duke of Burgundy from 1465 to 1477, ruled large parts of what is now Eastern France, Belgium and the western Netherlands from here, presiding over one of medieval Europe's most resplendent Renaissance courts. While some palatial residences from Charles' time remain, they are dwarfed by a cache of medieval churches that cram the city. Most notable is the cathedral, whose remarkably elegant tower – just shy

The Grote Markt - the main square - in Mechelen, the city in Belgium that has a number of links with the princes.

145

St Rombout's Cathedral in Mechelen, Belgium. The noted Tudor physician John Clement, who according to one theory was the grown-up Richard of Shrewsbury, is buried beside the church's high altar.

of 100 metres tall – rises over the pretty pastel-coloured merchants' houses that line the expansive market square, known in Flemish as the Grote Markt. The cathedral is dedicated to Saint Rombout, an obscure Irish saint who converted the heathens hereabouts to Christianity

Another view of St Rombout's Cathedral.

in the seventh century; some five centuries later, at the height of the mania for cathedral-building that gripped Europe in the High Middle Ages, construction began on this gargantuan church, which to this day houses the shrine that reputedly contains Rombout's earthly remains (his reliquary is paraded around the town on major feast days). At other

147

The High Altar in St Rombout's Cathedral in the Belgian city of Mechelen. According to one theory the noted Tudor physician John Clement, who is buried beside the altar, was in fact the grown-up Richard of Shrewsbury.

times the shrine rests behind the cathedral's magnificent High Altar, a Baroque masterpiece in black, white and gold that is the highlight of the building's interior (along with some extraordinary medieval panel paintings depicting Rombout's life).

148

Also buried near the High Altar are the remains of John Clement, one of the most prominent English physicians of the sixteenth century. He died in Flanders in 1572, one of the more prominent Catholic emigres who settled in the city of Leuven (Louvain), around 10 miles southeast of Mechelen, after fleeing from Elizabeth I's Anglican religious settlement. Although the standard biography of Clement gives his year of birth as 1500, and has him educated at St Paul's School in London and at Corpus Christi College, Oxford, an 'alternative' biography – championed by some – places his year of birth much earlier, in 1472; for the adherents of this 'alternative' theory claim that John Clement was in fact Richard of Shrewsbury, who was freed as a child from the Tower of London to take on a new life, and who emerged decades later to occupy a prominent position at the heart of Henry VIII's England.

The originator of this claim was Jack Leslau (1931–2004), an amateur art historian from London, who spent years (and thousands of pounds) putting flesh on his theory – which he derived from what he regarded as secret messages encoded by Hans Holbein into a painting made in 1527 of the family of Sir Thomas More. Leslau's theory has been expounded at length on websites and in books, and there is only space here to give a brief outline of it. Holbein's painting, which Leslau spent so long analysing, is entitled *Sir Thomas More and Family*, and depicts More wearing a red robe and surrounded by ten other figures, with an eleventh figure, his back turned to the artist, visible through an open doorway. This original work was destroyed by a fire in a Moravian castle in the eighteenth century but a copy survives, commissioned in 1593 by More's grandson from the Elizabethan artist Rowland Lockey; it is now hung in Nostell Priory, a Palladian country house near Wakefield – and Holbein's original study for the painting also survives, in Basel. For Leslau the focus of the painting is not Sir Thomas More, its ostensible subject, but a man who appears to his right, looking somewhat detached from the rest of the group – as if he has just entered the room unaware that people were posing for a portrait. This man is usually assumed to be John Harris, More's secretary. But Leslau asserts this figure is not Harris but is instead John Clement, who was tutor to Thomas More's children (in fact he married More's adopted daughter Meg Giggs in around 1526); he goes on to suggest that Holbein secreted in the painting several visual and verbal clues that reveal that Clement is in fact the grown-up Richard of Shrewsbury, given a new life and identity after being freed from the Tower of London.

These clues include the inscription above John Harris that reads 'Johanes heresius', which translates as 'John the rightful heir' – to the English crown, Leslau asserts; Harris (or Clement, or Richard, depending on the veracity of the theory) is also depicted higher than any other figure in the painting (including More), indicating – so Leslau believes – his elevated social status; and he carries a sword, which would be an unusual accoutrement for a servant, though not for a king. This 'mystery man' also holds a parchment; if what is pictorially represented is translated into French, then it could be said that 'il tient le parchemin' – 'he holds a parchment' – which in courtly French also means 'he holds the right and title of nobility'. Near his sword is a buckler – a warrior's status symbol – with a polished rim and spokes; in French the spoke of a wheel is 'rai' and the rim 'jante', which (Leslau asserts) is a split-homophone of 'régente' (king) – and 'le bouclier du régente', which translates as 'buckler of the king'. Numerous other clues abound, mostly taking the form of elaborate riddles, puzzles and word-plays that arise from the juxtaposition of people and objects in the painting, and largely invisible to those who do not have a close appreciation of the verbal dexterity of the French language. Leslau also focuses on a clock in the painting, which depicts a solar eclipse (the sun is a royal symbol of the house of York) and is shown with the window covering its winding mechanism open, suggesting that someone has been changing the time; according to Leslau, the waxing half moon in the dial shows that the 'mystery man' is only half his real age – and sure enough, John Harris was 27 when the painting was made, while Richard of Shrewsbury would have been 54.

Leslau's detractors suggest that the designation of John Harris as 'heir' probably refers to Harris being the rightful heir to More as a staunch Catholic, and point out that the Fleur-de-Lys design seen above Harris's head, which Leslau claimed was included to indicate that Harris had royal forebears, is actually part of the architectural design of the room. It is more difficult to explain away Clement's burial place beside the High Altar in Mechelen, a position normally reserved for the highest members of society. However, if John Clement really was Richard of Shrewsbury, then he would have been 98 years old when he died in 1571 – not impossible for the sixteenth century, but quite unlikely; Leslau's critics have also wondered whether it would have been likely that Thomas More would have let Holbein into such a potentially explosive royal and political secret in the first place. In his 1991 book

Richard III and the Princes in the Tower the historian A.J. Pollard called Leslau's extraordinary claims 'a brilliant flight of fancy'. Undaunted by such scepticism Leslau pressed on with his claim, maintaining that Edward Plantagenet was also released from the Tower in 1485, and grew up to become Sir Edward Guildford, Lord Warden of the Cinque Ports, Marshal of Calais, and the father of Jane Dudley, whose husband John Dudley was Duke of Northumberland and Lord Protector of England during the minority rule of Edward VI.

Until his death in December 2004 Leslau repeatedly petitioned the authorities to conduct a DNA test on the remains of both Guildford (who Leslau claims is buried in Chelsea Old Church) and John Clement to ascertain whether they were blood relations. Meanwhile the intriguing possibility that John Clement played a major role in the household of Sir Thomas More, who knew and protected his secret (though shared it with Holbein), has attracted at least one writer of historical fiction, Vanora Bennett – whose novel *Portrait of an Unknown Woman* is told from the perspective of More's independently-minded adopted daughter, Meg Giggs. She first encounters John Clement at the age of 9, when he becomes her tutor: 'a gentle giant with an eagle's nose and long patrician features [with] black hair and pale blue eyes with the sky in them … he taught us Latin and Greek letters by pinning them to archery targets in the garden and letting us shoot them through with arrows.' Later Clement admits to her who he really is, and she is forced to choose between him and Holbein as lovers and possible marriage partners; if Clement really was a grown-up Richard of Shrewsbury he would have been in his fifties at the time he wooed Meg – something that does not really come across in his characterisation in the novel.

Mechelen: Margaret of York and the Two Pretenders

If – *pace* Jack Leslau – Richard of Shrewsbury did not live in the Low Countries in the mid-sixteenth century as John Clement, perhaps he made an appearance in Mechelen much earlier. After the Yorkist defeat at Bosworth the city gained notoriety as a haven for Yorkist opposition to the new Tudor regime of Henry VII. This was down to the presence there of one of the most remarkable and formidable women of the age: Margaret of York, Duchess of Burgundy, the sister of Edward IV and

The Hof van Kamerijk, the former palace of Margaret of York in Mechelen, Belgium. Margaret was the sister of Edward IV and Richard III. It was from here that she championed the causes of the two pretenders to the throne of Henry VII.

Richard III, and the aunt of Edward and Richard Plantagenet. Margaret's modest palace, the Hof van Kamerijk, can be seen to this day in the centre of Mechelen, some 250 metres east of the Grote Markt on an architecturally undistinguished street named Keizerstraat; the palace was enlarged specifically for her when she took up residence there in 1477, but the building later became a Jesuit complex and is now the town's municipal theatre, and its somewhat plain façade gives little hint that this was once a palatial aristocratic home. According to the Irish historian Mary Hayden, Margaret was a woman 'skilled in intrigue' – and this capacity for scheming and plotting – as well as Margaret's fierce loyalty to the House of York – led to her supporting the two great 'pretenders' to the throne of Henry VII, namely Lambert Simnel and Perkin Warbeck, who both claimed at one time that they were Richard of Shrewsbury, and therefore had a better claim to the English throne than the Tudor usurper Henry VII. Their stories, mired as they are in as much controversy and debate as the fate of the princes themselves, make for compelling reading, and have been passionately debated by chroniclers and historians from their own time to the present day.

Margaret of York was born in 1446, either at Waltham Abbey in Essex or in Fotheringhay Castle in Northamptonshire, where her brother Richard was also born (sources differ, though the Richard III society believes it to be Waltham Abbey, and has installed a plaque there in her memory). Her childhood was spent in England, while her older brothers Edward and Richard sought exile from the bloody turbulence of the Wars of the Roses in the Low Countries – where Margaret was destined to spend much of her adult life. Later, Edward IV created a household for Margaret in Greenwich Palace. In 1465, when Count Charles of Charolais, the son of the Duke of Burgundy, was widowed on the death of his second wife, Isabelle of Bourbon, negotiations were begun for him to marry Margaret. These were duly concluded three years later and in June 1468 Margaret set off from Margate for the Low Countries, where she married Charles at Damme near Bruges. Nine years later Charles was killed in battle but Margaret, instead of returning to England, remained in Flanders, establishing her court at Mechelen and supporting Charles's daughter Marie (from his previous marriage to Isabelle) in her marriage to the son of the Holy Roman Emperor, Maximilian. After the Yorkist defeat at Bosworth and the change of dynasty in England, Margaret welcomed Yorkist exiles and plotters to Mechelen – among whom were supporters of Lambert Simnel and Perkin Warbeck.

It was Simnel who emerged first. In spite of Henry VII dealing swiftly with his rivals when he acceded the throne, rounding up all the young Yorkist claimants and placing them under supervision, within a year of his coronation the king found himself confronting a pretender in the form of a young boy whom members of the House of York were claiming as one of their own – and the rightful king of England. Yet the strange affair of Lambert Simnel is not as clear-cut as it initially seems. He (or his supporters) asserted at various times that he was both Richard of Shrewsbury and Edward, Earl of Warwick, the son of the executed Duke of Clarence. Edward was 10 years old at the time and would have been a firm candidate to inherit the throne on Richard III's death, had his father's attainder and execution for treason not debarred him; by contrast Richard of Shrewsbury would, by 1487, have been older – around 13. When the boy-pretender was unmasked as an impostor an extraordinary (and scarcely believable) story was put about that he was in fact neither of these contenders for the throne, but a low-born

Lambert Simnel after being crowned King of England in Dublin. Many theories surround this mysterious boy, who claimed at one point to be the grown-up Richard of Shrewsbury. From a 1910 Encyclopaedia Britannica. (*Source, Wikimedia Commons*)

urchin from Oxford named Lambert (or possibly John) Simnel who had been brought up by a priest who fancied himself a kingmaker. But was this a yarn spun by an embarrassed Tudor administration, who were fully aware of the boy's royal identity and that he actually posed a dangerous threat to the regime? All that seems certain is that a boy later called Lambert Simnel was crowned King of England in a ceremony at Christ Church Cathedral in Dublin on 24 May 1487, and that the rag-tag army of mercenaries from Ireland and the Low Countries that supported him was roundly defeated by Henry VII at the Battle of Stoke Field, fought near Newark in Nottinghamshire, a few weeks later. The chronicler Bernard André wrote one of a number of conflicting versions of these events. 'While the dire death of King Edward's sons was still a fresh wound,' he recounted,

> seditious men hatched another new crime … in their evil-mindedness they gave out that some base-born boy, the son of a baker or tailor, was the son of Edward IV. Thus, in accordance with the scheme they had hatched, rumour had it that Edward's second son had been crowned king in Ireland.

On hearing of the coronation, King Henry sent officials to investigate, but according to André, the lad, schooled with skill by men who were familiar

154

with Edward's ways, 'very readily replied to all the herald's questions …
he was so strongly supported, a large number had no hesitation to die for
his sake.'

The traditional version of Lambert Simnel's story is that this innocent
boy, sucked into a conspiracy by those who opposed the new Tudor order,
was born around 1475, the son of an Oxford tradesman named Thomas
Simnel (who was a baker, a joiner, a tailor or an organ-builder, depending
on which account you believe). Lambert's name was first mentioned in
an Act of Attainder against Edward IV's nephew John de la Pole, Earl of
Lincoln, one of the leaders of the rebellion that later gathered around
him. The attainder declared that the earl had,

> traitorously renounced, revoked and disclaimed his own said
> most natural sovereign liege lord the king, and caused one
> Lambert Simnel, a child of ten years of age, son of Thomas
> Simnel late of Oxford, joiner, to be proclaimed, set up and
> acknowledged king of the realm … to the great dishonor and
> shame of the whole realm.

It appears that young Lambert ended up in this position through falling
into the care of an ambitious Oxford priest named Richard Simons
(or Symons), who apparently, for no other reason than his own advancement
(and possibly his own amusement), taught the boy courtly manners and
bearing; Polydore Vergil recounts how Simons 'took Lambert to Oxford,
where he studied letters and with wonderful zeal began to acquire royal
manners, the goodly arts, and to memorise the royal pedigree so that,
when the need should arise, the common people might admire the boy's
character and more readily believe this lie.' In this the priest seems to have
succeeded, with contemporaries noting the boy's intelligence, courtly
manners and dignified appearance.

Exactly who the wily priest persuaded Lambert to impersonate
in Ireland is also somewhat fuzzy. Only Bernard André suggests he
impersonated Richard of Shrewsbury. Polydore Vergil maintains that
when Simons took the boy to Dublin the priest claimed that his charge
was in fact Edward, Earl of Warwick – and this seems a good opportunity
to summarise the life of this unfortunate boy, whose life and fate both
echoes and touches those of the princes. Edward was born on 25 February
1475 at Warwick Castle. After his father's execution he became a royal

ward; in 1481 Edward IV assigned Thomas Grey, the Marquess of Dorset, to be his guardian. But Grey fled to Brittany after the accession of Richard III and Edward, then 8 years old, was sent by Richard to Sheriff Hutton where he was brought up with other scions of the House of York. Two years later, after Richard's defeat at Bosworth Field, the boy found himself the prisoner of the victorious Henry VII, who, realising Edward's claim to the throne was more valid than his own, placed him in the Tower of London. There he remained, for the rest of his life; not surprisingly he has been called the 'third prince in the Tower'. This was the boy, then – somehow newly escaped or released from the Tower – whom (according to some sources) Yorkists assumed they were crowning in Dublin as their new king. The Burgundian chronicler Jean de Molinet, writing around 1504 or just before, was convinced, for one, writing of,

> Edward, son of the Duke of Clarence, who ... with the support of a number of barons of England ... decided after due debate to have himself crowned king, and to expel from his royal throne the Earl of Richmond [Henry VII], who was then in possession of the crown of England.

Not surprisingly Henry reacted to the trouble in Ireland by having the real Edward Earl of Warwick, his prisoner, paraded through the streets of London, to demonstrate to the populous that the boy in Dublin was an impostor. But the Earl of Lincoln, the boy's principal supporter, persisted with his scheme, crossing the Irish Sea and landing in Lancashire with an army from the Low Countries provided by his aunt, the Duchess of Burgundy. Disaster duly awaited them at Stoke Field, where Lincoln was killed (the exact site of this battle is disputed; a memorial stone at a ridge known as Burham Furlong marks the place where Henry VII raised his standard, though it lies on private land and is inaccessible to the public; there is also a memorial to the dead of the battle in the Churchyard at East Stoke village).

So who exactly was the boy crowned in Dublin? A low-born tradesman's son from Oxford? Edward, Earl of Warwick? Richard of Shrewsbury? Or an impostor, claiming to be either of these claimants to the throne? The historian John Ashdown-Hill has concluded that, contrary to general orthodoxy, he might actually have been Edward, Earl of Warwick, while it was Henry's prisoner in London who was the impostor or substitution of some kind. One piece of evidence for this flight-of-fancy was that Molinet wrote that 'one little branch [of the] ... royal tree had been nurtured among the fruitful and lordly shrubs of Ireland,' leading Ashdown-Hill to suggest that young Edward had been smuggled out of England to Ireland shortly after his father's execution, and had been raised by the fiercely loyal Yorkist, the Earl of Kildare. At one point, Ashdown-Hill suggests, Edward became a guest of Margaret of York at her palace in Mechelen, and there's a hint of this in the name that the boy captured at Stoke Field gave when he was captured – Lambert is the Patron Saint of Flanders. An even more outlandish suggestion is that Simnel was in fact Edward Plantagenet (who would have been 17 years old by the time of the Battle of Stoke Field), but no fifteenth-century chroniclers suggested this, and a document preserved in York and examined by John Ashdown-Hill states unequivocally that the Dublin king called himself Edward VI rather than V, making it highly unlikely that he was the older of the two princes, who presumably would have kept his original regnal number had he been restored to the throne. Whoever the boy captured at Stoke Field was – and he only seems to have been given the name Lambert Simnel after the battle – he was pardoned by Henry VII and was afterwards set to work as a turnspit in the royal kitchens. Later he was promoted to the position of the king's falconer and died in around 1525. Even here, though, confusion reigns; some sources suggest that the 'Dublin king' escaped from the bloody battle site at Stoke Field, making the turnspit an impostor, while others suggest that the putative king was killed on the battlefield and was replaced with Simnel afterwards. Part of the problem lies with the age of the boy at the centre of it all; according to the Act of Attainder against the Earl of Lincoln, the boy who became the royal turnspit was only 10 years old, while the Pretender crowned in Ireland was 15 – yet another layer of confusion in which the whole sorry tale of Lambert Simnel is smothered.

The tragic life story of Edward, Earl of Warwick, the 'third prince in the Tower', came to an end on 28 November 1499, when he was beheaded for treason on Tower Hill, after fourteen years in custody. The official reason given was that the earl – then aged 24, and according to some historians, mentally retarded in some way – had tried to escape, along with Perkin Warbeck, also languishing in the Tower after his exposure as a fellow pretender to the throne. (Some have suggested that an agent provocateur, planted among the jailers of the Tower, encouraged the two men to escape together, to give the government the excuse to rid themselves of the two main threats to the realm.) It is more likely that pressure to execute the

Earl of Warwick had come from Ferdinand and Isabella of Spain, whose daughter Catherine of Aragon was about to marry Henry VII's son Prince Arthur; they did not wish to see a man with such a powerful claim to the throne still living while their daughter was betrothed to the heir to the English crown.

As for Perkin Warbeck, he, like Lambert Simnel before him, was championed by Margaret of York from her Mechelen palace – but unlike Simnel, Warbeck's claim to the throne was much more believable, and many of his contemporaries, as well as historians, were, and are, willing to believe that he just might have been the person he claimed to be, namely Richard of Shrewsbury, the younger of the two princes.

Warbeck made his first appearance on the political scene at Cork in 1491, some four years after the apparent unmasking and defeat of Lambert Simnel at Stoke Field. He started off by announcing that he was a bastard son of Richard III, then he asserted that he was in fact Edward, Earl of Warwick, son of the Duke of Clarence, just as Lambert Simnel had; but then he changed his story again, and claimed that he was actually a grown-up Richard of Shrewsbury, an identity that he then stuck with. When he first voiced his claim in Ireland, local nobles rallied to his cause and he was recognised by several European rulers as Richard Plantagenet. In March 1492 he was welcomed as a visiting sovereign at the French court, but he fled to Flanders after Charles VIII agreed in the Treaty of Étaples that he would not to give refuge to any pretenders to the English throne. In her palace in Mechelen, Margaret of York recognised him as her long-lost nephew Richard, though how well she had actually known Richard before his incarceration in the Tower is a matter of debate. Later on, James IV of Scotland also recognised Warbeck as the rightful King of England and arranged for him to marry Lady Catherine Gordon, the daughter of one of Scotland's most prominent noblemen, George Gordon, the 2nd Earl of Huntly (of whom the poet George Gordon, Lord Byron was a descendant). The Archduke Maximilian, the ruler of the Low Countries, whose son was married to Margaret of York's stepdaughter, also formally endorsed Warbeck, and when he died shortly afterwards, Warbeck represented England at his funeral in Vienna. All of this created great alarm in Henry VII's England. In 1493 a report issued in the city of York (now kept in the city archives) noted that the city's mayor was concerned about 'the public noise and rumour [over] the king's enemies and rebels, being beyond the sea with the Lady Margaret,

Duchess of Burgundy,' and that a rebel named 'Richard, Duke of York, and second son to King Edward IV, late king of this realm, intends shortly to enter this the king's realm' – before calling the men of the city to arms. Henry VII, angered by Mechelen being such a haven for his enemies, put an embargo on trade with the Low Countries, and started rounding up Warbeck's key supporters in England, most notably Sir William Stanley, who was executed in February 1495. But by late 1497, with a number of failed invasion attempts behind him, including a landing in Cornwall and a siege laid to the city of Exeter, the game was up, and Warbeck was arrested near Taunton and brought before the king.

In 1493 Warbeck had explained his extraordinary life story in a letter to Ferdinand and Isabella of Spain. In it he detailed how he had been spared the murder suffered by his brother Edward, and had been released from the Tower to be handed over to a man who initially intended to kill him – but who, taking pity on his innocence, had preserved his life and made him swear on the sacrament not to disclose the true nature of his birth and lineage. But when he ended up in the custody of King Henry, Warbeck changed his story, and confessed that he was in fact the son of John Osbeck (or Warbeck), a minor official from Tournai, a town 30 miles southwest of Brussels, and that his impersonation of Richard of Shrewsbury had begun during his employment with a Breton merchant named Pregent Meno, who sold fabrics in Ireland. He was executed on 23 November 1499, after making a confession on the scaffold at Tyburn that he was not the son of Edward IV.

The conundrum as to who Perkin Warbeck actually was has exercised historians for centuries. Sir Francis Bacon maintained that his deceit was 'a finer counterfeit ... than Lambert Simnel. He was a youth of fine favour and shape,' and thought that he really was a son of Edward IV. Warbeck (like Simnel before him) did appear to possess a regal bearing, and a drawing of him in a French manuscript, *Receuil d'Arras*, shows that he bore a striking resemblance to Edward IV. Since Edward was in exile in the Low Countries in 1470 it is possible that Warbeck was his bastard son; others have claimed that his father was Richard III, also in exile there at the same time. Most bizarrely, the Archduke Maximilian posited that Warbeck was the bastard son of Margaret of York by the Bishop of Cambrai, who in 1498 acted as Margaret's emissary to London when she sought a reconciliation with Henry VII, and who specifically requested to meet with Warbeck in the Tower during his visit.

Fiction writers have used the compelling mysteries of Lambert Simnel and Perkin Warbeck to conjure up some wonderful, though in some cases rather far-fetched, yarns. In 2017 his story was told in the novel *The Player King* by the American children's writer known only as 'Avi'; this novel adheres to the conventional story of Lambert Simnel – the action unfolding in Oxford, Dublin and Stoke Field – and maintains that Simnel impersonated the Earl of Warwick, with the Princes in the Tower barely mentioned. One of the best retellings of Perkin Warbeck's story is *The Master of Bruges*, by the historical novelist Terence Morgan, which portrays Princes Edward and Richard still living in the Tower of London during the reign of Richard III, the boys being taught painting and drawing by the Flemish artist around whom the novel revolves. Edward, by that time, was too ill to roam around the city, but Richard cheerily accompanies the painter through the pressing streets of medieval London: 'the rumour-mongers were looking for two princes; had they used their eyes they might have seen one prince, alive and well and happy, wandering the streets of London with his tutor', the artist muses. Eventually the boy becomes an apprentice to William Caxton, 'slaving over a printing press [and carrying] newly printed books back to his afflicted brother at night.' Edward is captured and killed as Henry VII's forces storm the Tower after Bosworth Field, while Richard is spirited away to Bruges. There he begins a new life as 'Peterkin', and is adopted by Sir Edward Brampton, a prominent Yorkist exile, as his page (Brampton was a real-life figure who, according to Warbeck's confession, had once been his employer). After revealing who he is, Warbeck ends up wandering 'from monarch to monarch in Europe, looking for some support in his quest for truth and justice. Poor boy,' the artist sighs. 'I fear no good will come of it all.'

Philippa Gregory also plays on Richard of Shrewsbury's possible survival in the Low Countries in her novel *The White Queen* – in which Richard is sent away from the Westminster sanctuary to Flanders, while a hapless pageboy is sent to the Tower in his place and is later murdered in his bed beside Edward. 'Though I am now called Peter,' Richard later writes to his mother, 'the woman here, who is kind to me, calls me her little Perkin and I don't mind this.' Elizabeth muses that 'the boy who now answers to Peter will go quietly to school, learn languages, music and wait … he will be the weapon they do not know we have, the boy in hiding, the prince in waiting … he and his will haunt every king who comes after us, like a ghost.'

The Mysterious Case of the Bricklayer from Eastwell

Four hundred years ago the Moyle family ruled the roost in the bucolic part of Kent that lies just north of the town of Ashford. The first of the Moyles to rise to prominence was Sir Walter Moyle, who served as a lawyer during the reign of King Edward IV; in 1465 Sir Walter was one of the honoured guests who witnessed the coronation of Queen Elizabeth Woodville in Westminster Abbey. Half a century later, Sir Walter's grandson Sir Thomas Moyle was pursuing the same career, practicing and prospering during the reign of King Henry VIII. Sir Thomas had made his home in an unostentatious country house in the hamlet of Eastwell, which today lies just beyond the northern spread of Ashford. Today this dwelling goes by the name of Lake House, thanks to the artificial lake created in the nineteenth century whose waters lap at its garden; now in private hands, the house still has its original medieval Great Hall intact, from the time of its construction by one John de Criol in around 1300. Towards the end of his career Sir Thomas, a possessor of a sharp mind

Lake House in the Kent village of Eastwell, once the home of Sir Thomas Moyle. According to one story Moyle recruited the grown-up Richard of Shrewsbury as a labourer when his new manor house near by was under construction.

as well as a beautiful house, became involved in the legal wrangling surrounding Henry VIII's dissolution of the monasteries, and managed to divert some of the great wealth of those religious houses into his own coffers; with that new-found wealth he decided to build for himself a very grand house that was befitting of his wealth and status. That house was to be situated on a ridge of high ground a short distance away from Lake House, overlooking the village of Boughton Lees. This new house he named Eastwell Manor, after the scattered hamlet that his original home was part of. Construction of Sir Thomas's new manor house began in the early 1540s, as the money from the dissolved monasteries came flooding in. Over the ensuing centuries the house has been much altered – so much so that virtually nothing of Sir Thomas Moyle's original house now survives, and what's there today is really no more than a sham; a country house built in the 'Jacobethan' style popular with Victorian architects that is now a country house hotel and wedding venue.

But it's not Eastwell Manor that's the focus of this part of the story. Instead it's Sir Thomas Moyle's original house, Lake House, tucked into

Eastwell Manor, Kent. Now a country house hotel and much rebuilt over the centuries. According to one story the grown-up Richard of Shrewsbury worked as a labourer on the original manor house that stood here.

a wooded crease in the hills a ten minute walk away, and linked to Eastwell Manor by a short stretch of the long-distance footpath known as the North Downs Way, that commands our interest, for this is where the final trail of the princes in the Tower leads. Beside Lake House (which, unlike Eastwell Manor, keeps itself to itself, and is barely visible from many angles, hidden behind fortunate topography and clumps of trees) are the beguiling ruins of the church of St Mary the Virgin, once the Parish Church of the hamlet (barely a scattering of farms) of Eastwell. Owing to its current lachrymose state, this church finds itself cared for by a body known as the Friends of Friendless Churches. The ruination is recent; Queen Victoria was once a regular visitor to Eastwell Manor, as she gazed up from the frozen lake next to the church she would have glimpsed through the trees a fully functioning English country church. The building dates from the 1380s and was constructed right beside what is now Lake House, the most important house in Eastwell, which in due course became the home of the Moyles (today an impenetrable wall separates church and

The ruined church at Eastwell, Kent. According to one story Richard Plantagenet - either an illegitimate son of Richard III, or his grown-up nephew, Richard of Shrewsbury, the younger of the princes - is buried in the churchyard.

house). The styles adopted were Decorated and Perpendicular, but the original church was subjected to some enthusiastic Victorianisation in the nineteenth century, when the 9th Earl of Winchelsea added some stained glass that just happened to incorporate Edward IV's 'sun in splendour' emblem into its design, alongside various shields of local families. What caused the calamitous decline of the church into its current sorry state is unclear; one of Hitler's V2 rockets, blasting operations set off by troops during wartime training, and the chalk blocks used for the interior soaking up water from the adjacent lake have all been blamed. The final kibosh came in February 1951, when the roof collapsed during a gale; the nave and chancel were demolished seven years later, leaving only the fifteenth-century tower, the west wall and the adjacent eighteenth-century mortuary chapel standing. Marble monuments and the remaining stained glass were dispatched to a number of locations for safe-keeping, including the Victoria and Albert Museum, which became the custodian of the tomb chest of Sir Thomas Moyle and his wife, Katherine.

Much of the love and care that embraced the church at this time came from an Australian archaeologist, Mary Wentworth Kelly, who had been a frequent visitor to the church in the 1930s (motoring down from London in her Austin Seven, according to an article in *Kent Life* in 1964); when she saw the state of the church after the gale had done its work she was horrified and, gathering together a group of like-minded friends and parishioners, she set about clearing the nave of rubble and weeds. Aware of the legend that one Richard Plantagenet was buried in the church, she planted some white roses (for the House of York) and broom (known in Latin as *Planta Genista*, from where the Plantagenets derive their name) – and affixed a plaque to the most prominent tomb in what was once the nave (though by then was fully open to the sky); now corroded almost to illegibility, the plaque reads 'Reputed to be the Tomb of Richard Plantagenet, 22 December 1550'. In doing so Kelly ensured the survival of the legend of Richard Plantagenet of Eastwell for generations to come.

However, the tomb on which the plaque bearing the name 'Richard Plantagenet' is affixed is probably not that of Richard but of Sir Walter Moyle, the first prominent owner of the adjacent Lake House; badly-worn figures on the tomb depict a woman and children, and Richard Plantagenet of Eastwell died unmarried and childless – not so Sir Walter Moyle, whose wife Margaret bore him a large family. The earliest chronicler of Richard of Eastwell, a clergyman named Dr Thomas Brett, maintains that the exact

The tomb in the ruined church at Eastwell purporting to be that of Richard Plantagenet, who according to one theory was the grown-up Richard of Shrewsbury.

location of Richard's tomb within the church at Eastwell is unknown, so even using the word 'reputedly' on this tomb is a little too strong; in fact it seems that Mary Wentworth Kelly simply picked the most prominent tomb in the church on which to affix her plaque.

A close-up view of the tomb in the church at Eastwell.

Richard Plantagenet of Eastwell is a shadowy figure, to say the least; the legend that surrounds him is even more crepuscular than the dim twilight that, on winter afternoons, enfolds the wooded glade in which the ruins of St Mary's Church lie hidden. All that is known about Richard for certain is that a man of this name died in Eastwell on 22 December 1550, a date recorded in the local Parish register. Nearly two centuries later, on 1 September 1733, one Dr Thomas Brett, a clergyman from the town of Rye in East Sussex, wrote a letter to William Warren, the President of Trinity Hall, Cambridge, in which he described an extraordinary legend that had been told to him some thirteen years previously by the then Earl of Winchelsea (Lords of the Manor of Eastwell at the time, and descendants of the Moyles) and that had been handed down through generations of the earl's family. Dr Warren, intrigued though perhaps not convinced, later passed the letter on to an antiquary, Francis Peck, who published the contents in his miscellany, *Desiderata Curiosa*, and in the *Gentleman's Magazine* of June 1767. The legend outlined by Dr Brett maintained that in 1542, when Sir Thomas Moyle's great manor house over the hill from the church at Eastwell was under construction, one of the bricklayers labouring there was observed by Sir Thomas to be reading a book of Latin verse – a strange past-time for a bricklayer in those days, when reading and writing (especially in Latin) was largely the province of the upper classes. When questioned, the softly spoken labourer revealed that he was in fact the bastard son of King Richard III, hence the quality of his education and the high standards of his tastes in reading material. Taking Sir Thomas into his confidence, the bricklayer explained how some sixty-five years previously he had been taken to Richard's tent at Bosworth Field on the eve of that fateful battle, where he was told never to reveal his true identity should Richard lose. The following day, the young man – at the time, only around 15 years of age – observed the battle from a safe distance, as he had been instructed, and so duly watched his father die. Since that time he had lived in anonymity, a state enforced on him by the fear of being unmasked as the offspring of a man whom the Tudor regime vilified and reviled. Sir Thomas, intrigued by Richard's story, gave him permission to build a small cottage in the grounds of his new Eastwell estate, which may be the dwelling known as 'Plantagenet's Cottage' that still survives, though this building has been much modified over the centuries.

Though undoubtedly a fascinating story, that's what it remains – a story. Not a shred of evidence exists to confirm any aspect of it; and when published by Francis Peck the tale had been passed down by word of mouth through several generations, no doubt embellished and distorted with each telling. But Richard's story is undoubtedly compelling; popularised in the nineteenth century, it was fictionalised in several novels, including *The Last of the Plantagenets* by William Heseltine (1829), *The Secret Son* by W.B. Nichols (1944) and, more recently, *The Sprig of Broom* (1971) by the noted children's novelist Barbara Willard. Her story centres on a young boy, Medley Plashet, who, growing up in the dense forests of the Sussex Weald, discovers that his distant, secretive father – a forester and labourer – is none other than Richard Plantagenet, bastard son of a king, and that he, Medley – whose surname recalls his royal lineage – must 'hide the knowledge of his blood' just as he must hide the dagger that hangs at his belt, emblazoned with the letter 'P' and a crown, an heirloom that was a gift to Medley's father from his own father, King Richard III. An even more recent fictional incarnation of Richard comes in *Richard of Eastwell* by Mark J.T. Griffin, a self-published novel from 2006 that intriguingly blends the tradition that Richard of Eastwell was the son of Richard III with an even more curious notion: that Eastwell's Richard was in fact Richard of Shrewsbury, the younger of the two princes in the Tower, who (according to Griffin's narrative) was spirited from the Tower of London by a kindly Richard of Gloucester (away from Lord Buckingham's potentially murderous hands) after the death, from natural causes, of his older brother. In Griffin's narrative this Richard grew up to be a master stonemason, joiner and builder, who worked on the Rose Theatre in London and then on Henry VII's great new palace at Richmond; in fact Richard reveals his true parentage to an astonished Henry Tudor when the king is on his deathbed, and then, on his own deathbed, lets it be known to (an equally astonished) Sir Thomas Moyle that he is in fact the last Plantagenet, who has spent his life looking back on the time that he had lived as a young prince in the great royal palaces of London, brother and son to kings of England.

No wonder novelists have been drawn to Richard Plantagenet of Eastwell; he offers an unusually blank canvas for writers to fill. But the idea that Richard of Eastwell is not a son of King Richard III but is instead that king's nephew, born as Richard of Shrewsbury, is not new; in her 1992 book *The Princes in the Tower* the historian Alison Weir described this as 'a modern theory', but with no pointer as to how modern it actually is. In 2007 the historian David Baldwin came up with a yarn to top anything that few of his novelist forebears had concocted; his book *The Lost Prince: The Survival of Richard, Duke of York*, put evidential flesh on the theory that Richard of Eastwell and Richard of Shrewsbury were one and the same person. Baldwin draws the main inspiration for his idea from the fact that nothing is known of Richard of Eastwell before the year 1483, and that nothing is known about Richard of Shrewsbury after this date – so could they actually be one and the same person? What follows in *The Lost Prince* is a lot of supposition and conjecture. – a fair bit of 'are we allowing our imagination to run away with us?' and 'are we stretching credibility too far?' Baldwin spins an imaginative yarn, but his propositions are built on such shaky foundations that they are actually impossible to disprove; but for what they're worth, his arguments are summarised here.

King Richard III sired a number of bastard sons during the course of his relatively short life. All were styled 'of Gloucester' and were handsomely provided for by their father. Yet no records have survived of the son who became 'our' Richard, the bricklayer from Eastwell. Could this mean that Richard's parentage wasn't as he suggested? (Remember, in considering this, that there's no proof that Richard of Eastwell ever claimed to be of royal birth in the first place, and that it's entirely possible that the story of his birth has been spun out of nothing more than thin air.) In the narrative recorded by Dr Brett, Richard claimed to have been lodged as a boy in the home of a schoolmaster in the village of Lutterworth, an out-of-the-way place midway between Leicester and Rugby. In the Middle Ages this was an unremarkable farming settlement; today it's a Midlands commuter village, its dwellings gently shaken hour-by-hour by the traffic that pounds away on the nearby M1. By chance, Lutterworth turned out to be very close to the site of the Battle of Bosworth Field, allowing the boy to meet with King Richard on the eve of the battle, and, on the following day, to watch it unfold from a safe distance. Baldwin's contention, that the boy who watched the battle was Richard of Shrewsbury, spirited from the Tower of London soon after the death (from natural causes) of his sickly older brother, and sent by those in the know to grow to maturity in the backwater of Lutterworth, draws credibility (he claims) from the fact that the Manor of Lutterworth was held at the time by the Greys of Groby, the family of Elizabeth Woodville's first husband, the Lancastrian knight Sir John Grey of Groby, who was killed at the Battle of Towton; his family would have been sympathetic to the Woodville cause and would have been happy to shelter a scion of that family. When defeat came, Baldwin maintains that the prince – who would then have been six days past his twelfth birthday – was spirited away from the blood-soaked battle field and delivered into the care of a small group of Richard's closest confidants, namely Sir Francis Lovell, of Minster Lovell near Oxford, and Humphrey and Thomas Stafford, of Grafton in Worcestershire. These young nobles did not – as might have been expected of men of their rank and loyalty – take part in the Battle of Bosworth. Was this so that they would be sure to remain alive so that they could perform the secret task that Richard had entrusted to them – namely, to take his young nephew into their care, and to deliver him, as Richard had already planned, to Colchester in Essex, and the safe hands of the abbot of St John's Abbey? This is certainly what David Baldwin suggests happened. Colchester at that time was a well-known refuge for Yorkist dissidents, and Richard of Shrewsbury would have joined the group of boys who already lodged there in the abbot's care, with few if any eyebrows raised. There Richard would have lived and grown in anonymity, continuing his education with the other boys hunched over their desks in the abbey's schoolroom.

Richard apparently continued to live in Colchester even after his education at the hands of the abbot was finished. Baldwin has ascertained that a 'yeoman or labourer' named Richard Grey was living in the city in 1512, working in St John's Abbey, and suggests that Richard of Shrewsbury may have taken this name as an adult as a gesture, known only to himself, acknowledging his mother's lineage; yet, as Baldwin goes on to admit, Richard Grey was a very common English name during this era. Could the Richard Grey of Colchester really have been Richard of Shrewsbury? And on the dissolution of St John's Abbey in 1538 by Henry VIII's commissioners, when Richard was put out of work, did he really end up some four years later knocking on the door of what is now Lake House, in Eastwell, wondering if Sir Thomas Moyle could find him employment in the building of his new manor house? There is, of course, no way of proving the notion that Richard of Eastwell was the younger of the Princes in the Tower. But there is no way of disproving it, either. And we can leave Richard of Eastwell's story with a final flight of fancy: as he worked on the house that was to become Eastwell Manor, did he ever put down his bricks and his books and take time off to travel the twelve miles across the North Downs to Canterbury, there to gaze upon his own portrait in the Royal Window in the city's great cathedral, a memory in stained glass of a former life that, by then, only he was aware of?

In 1708 a grisly discovery was made in the great manor house at Minster Lovell, situated in the deep Cotswold countryside west of Oxford; it was a skeleton, sitting at a table in an alcove that had been bricked up nearly two centuries before. No one was sure who the bones belonged to, but their owner has always been assumed to be Lord Lovell, the confidant of Richard III whom Baldwin asserts accompanied the young Richard of Shrewsbury to sanctuary in Colchester after the Battle of Bosworth. It is Baldwin's theory that Lovell was done in by agents of Henry VII at his home in around 1487, simply because he knew too much about the survival of the younger of the princes; his upright body was left to decay for the next two centuries behind a wall that the agents (competent bricklayers as well as assassins) built behind them. While this might fit with Baldwin's theory that Lovell was murdered because of the devastating secret he knew, proof is of course hard to come by; it is not even certain that the skeleton in the alcove was actually that of Sir Francis Lovell, and the causes and circumstances of this unfortunate figure's death are, of course, even hazier – like the fate of the princes in the Tower themselves.

Bibliography and Further Reading

Fiction and Plays

Beattie, Andrew, *Blood Royal*, (YouthPLAYS, Los Angeles, 2014)

Bennett, Vanora, *Portrait of an Unknown Woman*, (Harper Collins, London, 2007)

Darwin, Emma, *A Secret Alchemy*, (Headline, London, 2008)

Gregory, Philippa, *The White Queen*, (Simon and Schuster, London, 2009)

Griffin, Mark T.J., *Richard of Eastwell*, (Amazon Media, 2011)

Morgan, Terence, *The Master of Bruges*, (Macmillan, London, 2010)

Shakespeare, William, *Richard III*, (Simon and Schuster, New York, 2018; first published 1597)

Tannahill, Reay, *The Seventh Son*, (Headline, London, 2001)

Tey, Josephine, *The Daughter of Time*, (Heinemann, London, 1951; republished 2009 by Arrow)

Weir, Alison, *A Dangerous Inheritance*, (Hutchinson, London, 2012)

Non-Fiction

Ashdown-Hill, John, *The Dublin King*, (The History Press, Stroud, 2015)

Baldwin, David, *The Lost Prince: The Survival of Richard of York*, (Sutton Publishing, Stroud, 2007)

Baldwin, David, *Elizabeth Woodville: The Mother of the Princes in the Tower*, (Sutton Publishing, Stroud, 2012)

Baldwin, David, *Richard III*, (Amberley Publishing, Stroud, 2012)

Hicks, Michael, *Edward V: The Prince in the Tower*, (The History Press, Stroud, 2003)

Higginbottom, Susan, *The Woodvilles: The Wars of the Roses and England's Most Infamous Family*, (The History Press, Stroud, 2013)

Higgs, John, *Watling Street,* (Weidenfeld & Nicolson, London, 2017)

Hindle, Brian, *Medieval Roads and Tracks*, (Shire Publications, Princes Risborough, 1982; republished 1998 by Shire Archaeology)

James, Jeffrey, *Edward IV: Glorious Son of York,* (Amberley Publishing, Stroud, 2015)

Jenkyns, Richard, *Westminster Abbey: A Thousand years of National Pageantry,* (Profile Books, London, 2004)

Lewis, Matthew, *The Survival of the Princes in the Tower: Murder, Mystery and Myth,* (The History Press, Stoud, 2017)

Mancini, Dominic, *The Usurpation of Richard III,* (Sutton Publishing, Stroud, 1984, translated by C.A.J. Armstrong; originally written 1483)

More, Thomas, *The History of King Richard III,* (Dalcassian Publishing/ CreateSpace Independent Publishing Platform, 2017; originally published 1513-1518)

Orme, Nicholas, *The Education of Edward V,* (published in the *Bulletin of the Institute of Historical Research*, vol LVII No.136, London, November 1984)

Pollard, A.J., *Richard III and the Princes in the Tower,* (Sutton Publishing, Stroud, 1991)

Potter, Jeremy, *Good King Richard? An Account of Richard III and his Reputation, 1483-1983,* (Constable, London, 1983)

Seward, Desmond, *Richard III: England's Black Legend,* (Country Life Books, London, 1982; republished by Pegasus, 2017)

Shoesmith, Ron, and Andy Johnson, (eds) *Ludlow Castle: Its History and Buildings* (Logaston Press, Herefordshire, second edition 2006)

Tanner, Lawrence, and William E. Wright, *Recent Investigations Regarding the Fate of the Princes in the Tower,* (published in *Archaeologia*, Volume 84, London, 1935; republished online in 2011 by Cambridge University Press)

Unwin, Richard, *Westminster Bones: The Real Mystery of the Princes in the Tower,* (CreateSpace Independent Publishing Platform, 2015)

Weir, Alison, *The Princes in the Tower,* (The Bodley Head, London, 1992; republished as *Richard III and the Princes in the Tower* by Vintage, 2014)

Weir, Alison, *Elizabeth of York: The First Tudor Queen,* (Jonathan Cape, London, 2013)

Williamson, Audrey, *The Mystery of the Princes,* (Sutton Publishing, Stroud, 1978; republished 2010 by Amerbley Publishing)

Wroe, Ann, *The Perfect Prince: The Mystery of Perkin Warbeck and His Quest for the Throne of England,* (Random House, London, 2003)

Index